JACOB WALLENBERG: MY SON ON THE GALLEY

Some other books from Norvik Press

Sigbjørn Obstfelder: *A Priest's Diary* (translated by James McFarlane)
Annegret Heitmann (ed.): *No Man's Land. An Anthology of Modern Danish Women's Literature*
P C Jersild: *A Living Soul* (translated by Rika Lesser)
Sara Lidman: *Naboth's Stone* (translated by Joan Tate)
Selma Lagerlöf: *The Löwensköld Ring* (translated by Linda Schenck)
Villy Sørensen: *Harmless Tales* (translated by Paula Hostrup-Jessen)
Camilla Collett: *The District Governor's Daughters* (translated by Kirsten Seaver)
Jens Bjørneboe: *The Sharks* (translated by Esther Greenleaf Mürer)
Johan Borgen: *The Scapegoat* (translated by Elizabeth Rokkan)
Jørgen-Frantz Jacobsen: *Barbara* (translated by George Johnson)
Janet Garton & Henning Sehmsdorf (eds. and trans.): *New Norwegian Plays* (by Peder W.Cappelen, Edvard Hoem, Cecilie Løveid and Bjørg Vik)
Gunilla Anderman (ed.): *New Swedish Plays* (by Ingmar Bergman, Stig Larsson, Lars Norén and Agneta Pleijel)
Knut Hamsun: *Selected Letters 1879-1898* (ed. Harald Næss and James McFarlane)
Michael Robinson (ed.): *Strindberg and Genre*

The logo of Norvik Press is based on a drawing by Egil Bakka (University of Bergen) of a Viking ornament in gold, paper thin, with impressed figures (size 16x21mm). It was found in 1897 at Hauge, Klepp, Rogaland, and is now in the collection of the Historisk museum, University of Bergen (inv.no. 5392). It depicts a love scene, possibly (according to Magnus Olsen) between the fertility god Freyr and the maiden Gerðr; the large penannular brooch of the man's cloak dates the work as being most likely 10th century.

Cover illustration designed by A and V Vargo.

JACOB WALLENBERG

My Son on the Galley

Edited and translated by Peter Graves

Norvik Press
1994

Peter Graves is Head of the Dept of Scandinavian Studies in the University of Edinburgh.

Original title: *Min son på galejan*. First published 1781.

British Library Cataloguing in Publication Data
Data available

ISBN 1-870041-23-2

First published in 1994 by Norvik Press, University of East Anglia,
Norwich, NR4 7TJ, England
Managing Editors: James McFarlane and Janet Garton

Norvik Press has been established with financial support from the University of East Anglia, the Danish Ministry for Cultural Affairs, The Norwegian Cultural Department, and the Swedish Institute.

Printed in Great Britain by Biddles Ltd, Guildford, Surrey.

Contents

Introduction

'I am curious and inquisitive but I cannot abide work. I love common sense but I hate learning. I read a lot and learn little, going in more for show than for substance. I have gathered for myself a pretty useless storehouse of entertaining and decorative items and I have left nourishment and enrichment to others. I have Ovid's rules of love at my fingertips but I have never been bothered about how many paragraphs there are in our law-code. Ask me about Horace and Catullus and you'll find me full to overflowing with their immodest verses but if it is a case of saying what St. Augustine wrote, *digito compesco labellum* (I put my finger to my lips). I can converse well enough with a French postillion or an English sailor but stick the Psalms of David or the Acts of the Apostles in Greek under my nose and you'll see the sort of fellow I am. In short, of all the honest ways of making a living in this realm there is not a single one that I am suited to – in spite of all my fancy words – unless I'm prepared to follow the example of the common herd and find any old occupation without worrying how it is to be performed. What's more, I think I can see all the signs of a good heart within me and I love all the obligations imposed by morality as long as they do not directly conflict with my pleasures. But as soon as that happens I must admit that feelings throw reason out of the window.'

Thus Jacob Wallenberg characterizes himself in a letter to a friend. With its wit and exaggeration, its deprecating modesty about his own learning, its insistence on common sense and, above all, its mixture of the humorous and the serious, it is a typical piece from the pen of the author of *Min son på galejan* (My Son on the Galley), the wonderfully funny travel journal that is one of the few texts from the Swedish 18th century that can still reach out and enchant a general audience. But before accepting the flippancy of Wallenberg's assessment of himself in the letter as the whole story one should go on to read, for instance, the mighty prayers in Chapter X of the First Finnish Expedition.

Jacob Wallenberg's life was short but active. Born in Östergötland in 1746 he was one of the many children of a minor law officer. (It is from Jacob's elder brother Marcus that the financial dynasty is descended.) He passed through the grammar school in Linköping with high praise and promise and arrived in Uppsala as a student in 1763. His money ran short after just one term and he became a private tutor in Västervik until he was able to return to Uppsala in 1765. Once again his time there was limited and in the autumn of 1766 he moved to Gothenburg as tutor to the sons of Martin Holterman, a director of the Swedish East India Company and a man of wealth and influence.

In Gothenburg Wallenberg landed on his feet. He immersed himself, as he had also done in Uppsala, in the life of the literary and drinking societies so typical of the age, wrote a good deal of occasional verse and thrived in the cosmopolitan atmosphere. In the spring of 1769 his attachment to the Holterman family enabled him to make his own Grand Tour, the first half of it with a son of the family but thereafter alone. It took him via Copenhagen to Hamburg, Amsterdam, Paris and London, and it resulted in a short travel narrative with a long, satirically intended but pompously youthful title:

A True Account of a Journey Beginning in the Royal Port and Dockyard of Kongsbacka . . . (and so on for a full page).

A True Account did not appear in print during Wallenberg's lifetime; nor for that matter did *My Son on the Galley*. *A True Account* is a very uneven production that swings backwards and forwards between parody of other travellers such as Linnaeus, satire of the nations visited, and frequent outbursts in the French Classical manner of which Wallenberg would clearly love to have been a master. Fortunately his strengths lay elsewhere, and there are parts of *A True Account* that truly merit its title. Its author's eye is observant, his sympathies active, his interests wide and his moral sense wide-awake. Wallenberg is anything but a prig but he is shockable and much that he sees shocks him. His portrait of London is particularly unflattering:

'London is the ugliest town I have ever seen. The conglomeration of black houses, great and small mingled together, the narrow crooked streets perpetually covered in filth, the unhealthy and foggy air and the ragged and undisciplined mob fill a stranger rather with horror than with wonder and delight.'

Just before his Grand Tour, thanks again to the support of the Holtermans, Wallenberg had taken the necessary examinations and been ordained in order to enable him to take up the post of ship's chaplain on the Swedish East India Company ship *Finland* at the remarkably young age of 23. Unlike its much larger Dutch, English and French counterparts which acquired territory as part of their ambition to achieve trading monopolies with the Orient, the Swedish East India Company was satisfied with trade alone. The company had been founded in 1731 largely on the initiative of foreign merchants prominent among whom was the Scot Colin Campbell who had exiled himself to Sweden to evade debts incurred when the South Sea Bubble burst but who honourably enough made provision for those debts to be paid off in his will 30 years later. Sailing mainly out of Gothenburg, the company enjoyed a chartered monopoly on trade between Sweden and China and the East Indies for 82 years until it was dissolved in 1813, having by then made some 132 voyages in 40 ships. The outward cargo was often iron, the homebound cargoes above all tea, silk and china which, at least in the first fifty years of the company's life, brought a handsome profit as well as a taste of exotic luxury to more affluent Swedes.

Profitable the voyages may have been but they were certainly not without considerable danger as Wallenberg's account, particularly of the early stages of his maiden voyage in the North Sea and Atlantic, makes quite clear. The company lost eight ships during its existence. The round trip from Gothenburg to Canton and back would normally last 17-18 months, taking the ships round the north of Scotland before they turned south and headed for the Dutch East India Company settlement at the Cape of Good Hope. As Wallenberg mentions, it was not unusual for this outward leg of the voyage to include a call at Cadiz, the purpose of which might be to acquire the silver pieces of eight that served as international currency or to replace sick or deceased members of the crew. The result of the visit often seems to have been to provide the ship's doctor with work in the form of cases of venereal disease.

Wallenberg made three voyages to the Far East in all: 1769-71, 1772-73 and 1774-75. On the first of these voyages he wrote much of *My Son on the Galley* and on the last of them he wrote his biblical drama *Susanna* which, although initially pronounced unstageable, became and remained for many years a popular play particularly in the repertoire of provincial companies. It was quite probably this drama that induced the theatre-mad King Gustav III to appoint him to a parish living. Thus, in 1777, he was given the parish of Mönsterås in Småland and resided there for the rest of his short life as, by all accounts, a humane and rather strict minister. (A manuscript collection of his sermons was discovered in the library of Nordiska museet as recently as 1961: they cover the whole of his career and the lighter side of Wallenberg's nature is not apparent.) His early death in 1778 can possibly be attributed to typhus.

My Son on the Galley (the strange title is a reference to a quotation in Molière's *Les fourberies de Scapin* – 'What the devil was he supposed to be doing on that galley?' – that seems to have become a set phrase in Sweden) is an account of the eight-and-a-half month outward voyage that took Wallenberg to Canton in September 1770, at which point he simply breaks off – in spite of having promised to continue and even having written the number of the following but absent chapter in the fair copy of his manuscript. It is somehow completely appropriate. Boredom, loss of interest, doubts about the suitability of such a production by a man of the cloth – whatever it was that prompted the abrupt break it shows critical acumen, for *My Son on the Galley* is just the right length as it is and stops before the seam is worked out. Those parts of the book that were written underway were, according to Captain Ekeberg of the *Finland* (who published his own account of the voyage), passed round sheet by sheet as reading material for Wallenberg's travelling companions; some of it undoubtedly appeared in the *Swedenborgian Post*, a journal of which the young ship's pastor produced two numbers for the amusement and edification of those aboard.

Amusement and edification are the keys to *My Son on the Galley* and they are present in equal parts. It is easy to allow the drastic and hail-fellow-well-met tone, the grand exaggeration and splendid grotesqueness, the burlesque of the drinking scenes, the manifest randiness of the young author and his perhaps inevitable interest in vomit to draw attention away from the moral seriousness that exists on almost every page. That the mixture of the humorous and the serious was as characteristic of the author as of his book is revealed by a number of near contemporary anecdotes and memoirs. According to P.D.A.Atterbom, whose father-in-law Nils Adolf af Ekenstam had sailed on the *Finland* on the 1769-71 voyage to the East Indies, Ekenstam described Wallenberg as 'not only a jolly and entertaining social companion but also an upright pastor endowed with great gifts as a preacher – far more strict and scrupulous in his habits and far more deeply Christian in the earnestness of his convictions than many people assumed they could gauge from the (often far-fetched) freedom of the humour in his celebrated travelogue'. Another anecdote puts the emphasis the other way round. On his visit to the Cape the German settlers, who had no pastor of their own, invited Wallenberg to hold a Lutheran service for them in German: 'And he did so, as well as preaching to them. But he was unable to win the approval of the Reformed populace (who demand such earnestness and exemplary conduct from a minister) since he was found after the service that very same day playing at cards with various minor gentlemen; the honorarium for his preaching was therefore only 100 riksdaler whereas it might otherwise have been 200.'

Manners and morals, then, are as much Wallenberg's field as humour and it is not merely in the externals of chapter headings and Latin tags that he reveals the influence of the moralizing journals in the tradition of Dalin's *Argus* and back through it to Addison and Steele's *Spectator*. Like these predecessors, Wallenberg is propagating a bourgeois ideal of a dispassionate, civilized, tolerant and Christian citizen – and that is a citizen who in Wallenberg's eyes will undoubtedly be a Lutheran Swede, for our pastor is nothing if not a patriot. The Swede at his normal best, he feels, steers the sensible middle course between the fopperies of the French and the blunt crudity of the Dutch, just as the Swedish church avoids the extremes of the Jesuits and the Dutch Reformed deacons alike. In general, the Dutch, the English and the Danes do not score highly; the Germans and the French do a little better; Swedes are best advised to stand by their 'svenskhet' and to avoid imitating any of them. Wallenberg is opinionated and his narrative is all the livelier for it but, irrespective of whether his attribution of characteristics to nations is accurate or not (and many of his attributions show how historically stable such national stereotypes are), there lies behind it all a genuine concern and an appeal for humanity and common-sense: he has no sympathy with the rapacious aspects of European colonialism, stresses moderation in drink and sex, demonstrates the tastelessness of marriages for money with an age gap that is wide, deplores the sexual exploitation of black women by white colonists, reviles greed, gluttony, envy and much else. Nor is there anything plodding about his condemnations – they are all done with vigour and verve and a keen eye for the gross and ridiculous.

As a moralist Wallenberg is in the fortunate position of both having his cake and eating it. On the one hand he is a quite genuine moralist; on the other, with his humour and exaggeration, he is able to parody the same moralizing attitudes and journals that provide much of the source of his writing. Furthermore, it is impossible to separate the travel writer in Wallenberg from the moralist. His occasional forays into natural history, scenic description, demography or whatever are more often than not parody of the disciples of Linnaeus and the scientific school of travel writing and he passes over them quickly in order to return to his central point of interest: man and his moral nature – the shark, as one of the chapters reveals, is soon swallowed up by a discourse on the shark-like attributes of mankind.

Since even a number of recent histories of literature have categorized *My Son on the Galley* as a 'comic novel' it is worth emphasizing that it is not a novel – though comic it certainly is. In so far as it is possible to check the reliability of facts and the actual course of events (in, for instance, Captain Ekeberg's account of the voyage), Wallenberg's claim that 'what I am writing about are real events' is fully justified. The events themselves are, in any case, often of secondary importance and serve as no more than the springboard from which Wallenberg launches himself into humorous and/or moral digressions – which are actually not digressions but the very substance of the book. Which is not to say that *My Son on the Galley* does not have a good deal in common with the 18th century novel. Nils Afzelius, who studied Wallenberg's travelogue against a background of contemporary Swedish and European literature in order to place it in terms of genre and influence, rightly suggested that the book rests firmly on the Linnean tradition of factual travel writing and that 'it is around that solid trunk that Wallenberg's imagination has climbed, produced its shoots and flowered'. There are also, Afzelius pointed out, many other elements. The importance of the weekly moralizing journal has already been mentioned: both form and content of many of the chapters in *My Son on the Galley* are strongly reminiscent of the more vigorous essays to be found in the journals. Then, not least of the unique qualities of Wallenberg's text, there is the way in which the Bacchanalian tradition of literary drinking societies after the manner of, for instance, Bellman's 'Order of Bacchus' has been fused together with the other elements: much of the verse with which Wallenberg peppers his text (and not a little of the prose) belongs to this sphere of literary social life. It is a life which Wallenberg himself had enthusiastically taken part in during his time in Uppsala and Gothenburg. Among foreign influences Afzelius finds Sterne of much less importance than has sometimes been suggested whereas Scarron and the whole French tradition of the 'voyage comique' together with Henry Fielding have provided Wallenberg with important stimuli.

My Son on the Galley soon captured an audience. No fewer than 25 editions of it have appeared in one form or another, including a modern paperback edition and a large-print version for the visually impaired. Extracts from it have appeared in anthologies too numerous to mention. The work was not published during Wallenberg's lifetime but he clearly allowed it to circulate among friends and them to make copies. The result was that when the first printed edition appeared in 1781, three years after Wallenberg's death, it was based on such a copy and not on Wallenberg's own manuscript. Marcus Wallenberg, Jacob's elder brother, made an unsuccessful legal attempt to suppress the publication ostensibly on the grounds that he owned his late brother's manuscripts and was preparing proper and reliable editions but, reading between the lines, the suspicion has to be that he felt it necessary to try to protect his brother's reputation as a man of the cloth. That Marcus Wallenberg's worries on this score were not entirely unreasonable may be seen from various contemporary references that, while usually expressing appreciation of the book, voice surprise that it should be the literary offspring of a minister. *My Son on the Galley* has been translated into German twice (1783 and 1975) and also into Italian (1971). Only extracts have previously appeared in English.

June 1993 P.G.

Min Son På Galejan,

eller

En Ostindisk Resa,

innehållande

Fi[illegible]gt Allehanda Bläckhorns-kram,

samlat

På Skeppet Finland,

Som afseglade från Götheborg i December 1769,

samt

återkom därsammastädes i Junio

1771,

af

Nedanstående med den röda Mössan.

Trykt i år

My Son on the Galley

or

An East Indian Journey

Containing

All Sorts of Scraps and Scribblings

Collected

Aboard the Ship Finland

Which sailed from Gothenburg in December 1769
and
returned there in June
1771

by
the Figure below with the red Cap

Printed in the year

The First Finnish Expedition
From Gothenburg to Norway

Chapter I

Parturiunt montes - - -[1]

In the days when L - - - won more fame with a few strokes of the pen than he had ever earned money with his mason's trowel; in the days when Colonel P – made himself a name as an honest man by a piece of trickery; in the days when Swedenborgian spirits were revealed in a Gothenburg court report; in the days when the Grand Vizier's parrot as well as his whole harem was captured at Khotin by General Golitsyn and the Russian eagle seemed destined to fly to the moon, or – what amounts to the same thing – to sail to Constantinople; in the days when the filth on the London streets was at its deepest and Englishwomen clattered loudest in their pattens[2]; in short, in the golden autumn of 1769, I – your present author – was commanded to present myself aboard the Swedish East India Company ship *Finland* which was ready to sail for Canton under the command of Captain C.G.Ekeberg.

We mustered but were given a further week's breathing-space to increase our old debts ashore. We could still drink with our friends, still wet the hand of some beloved Celinde with a parting tear, still be at the receiving end of conjugal lectures. Our patrons and acquaintances entertained us royally, presumably as an investment.

Everywhere there were kind hosts and happy faces for they knew that they would soon be rid of us and that anyone who treats an East Indiaman to two drinking bouts on his departure will receive fifteen in exchange at his homecoming.

Chapter II

CONCERNING THE PLEASURES OF THE KLIPPAN INN.

Vina bibant homines, animalia caetera fontes – Ovid.[3]

On the morning of the 8th December, even before that early riser Master N. and his journeymen had begun to hammer out the neighbourhood matins on their copper pans, I received a visit from the Company watchman. He arrived swinging his legs in a right watchmanly fashion and said that the wind was fair and we must to sea. Well, Father Watchman, so be it. I yawned a couple of times and threw on my clothes, bidding farewell to my lonely bachelor abode without much heartache. What an advantage it is not to be troubled by a whining wife on such occasions!

Outside the door I happened upon a host of East India friends who had received the same orders.

At once with lengthened step to Stibergs Lea we hastened,
Though piles of dirt reached halfway up our legs.
Our sorrowing eyes back on the town were fastened
But choice is small when mallets pummel pegs.
  Silken cloaks, capes and sweethearts!
  Susanna, Cloris and Eliza!

Farewell, alas, farewell! Though your lover now departs
In his heart you are as dear as money to a miser!
A final kiss we blow towards your bowers,
Faithful shall we stay through all the absent hours!
  At least to the Cape.

At last we managed to wade our way through Masthugget and our dear Klippan hove into view. We were still considering whether we should take a breather there for a while when good old Carnegie anticipated our wishes.[4] That very day he was taking special trouble to snap up East Indiamen; nor did he let us get away but, taking us by the arm, he uttered the following altruistic address: 'Gentlemen, you are not permitted to take money out of the country – that's against the King's regulations. Ik hap good red wine, capons, hares, pudding – *What ye please, gentlemen – – A toast for your sweethearts, before you are going away.*'

It would have taken the soul of a bear to make any objection to an offer accompanied by so many well-roasted reasons and supported into the bargain by a glance from *the young mistress herself, who stood smiling behind.* Not to mention little Stina, whose neat ankle was placed as if in ambush at the kitchen door. We friends stormed the door, in through the kitchen patting Stina as we passed. We occupied the biggest room with the noble intention of entrenching ourselves there behind an insuperable rampart of bowls and bottles. I followed the crowd and went too, having learned – by means of *a posteriori* arguments – from my schoolmaster in my youth the lesson:

Ulula cum lupis, cum quibus esse cupis.[5]

I shall never forget how the dirt of Masthugget still clung to our heels and how the full length of our booted hindpaws left lifesize imprints on the floor at every step. Mine host did his best, mine hostess skipped on ever lighter feet, and the spit turned more and more merrily. There was already a hare on the table; it was followed by a capon and, in between, the whole earth appeared in the form of a globe-shaped pudding. But what use is dry land if it is not watered by the sea? A veritable inlet of punch was set down alongside the globe, and here and there a stream of the Red Sea could be seen flowing into a glass. The sky might have been overcast outside but in here sunshine played on every face. Our parting from Gothenburg might have put melancholy furrows on our faces but Carnegie knew the secret of removing them. In short:

> Goodbye, last farthing! Proud on the table stood
> A mighty vessel, the tavern's boast of boasts,
> From which we imbibed a joyful stream of toasts
> Till cares were drowned, for now if not for good.
> To hell with sweetheart, friends and kin,
> All are forgotten as we drink,
> Bottles clink,
> Comrades wink,
> Songs sink,
> Drunk as a tink, tiddly -
> pom, pom, pom, tiddlypom.

In spite of it all we stayed fairly sober, and if anyone had a little trouble in walking it can be put down to the sealegs that sailors cannot avoid adopting aboard ship where they have to walk unevenly because of the roll. No, East Indiamen aren't the worst kind of fellows by any means. Ask at any inn – or among the ladies – and you'll hear what a good name they have.

Finland, like *Prins Gustav*, had meanwhile anchored off Älvsborg, but without firing a salute since she had too much respect for the herring to show any to the Commandant.[6] So we were in no hurry. Mine host entertained us until late in the evening and wore the same satisfied expression as a pedlar in Gränna when he sells half a barrel of rotten herrings to a farmer's wife at a halfpenny each. Then, so as not to risk our legs, he ferried us aboard in his own boat.

Chapter III

CONCERNING A CURIOUS KIND OF SHIP'S RAT

– – – *nascetur ridiculus mus* – Horat.[1]

Here, below the Älvsborg fortress, the ships remained at anchor for a full fortnight waiting for a favourable wind. However hot about the ears it may have been in 1720 when Tordenskiold's fleet was thundering away outside with its 48-pounders, it was all the colder now.[7] The Christmas frost up there in that stationary Finland near the North Pole could scarcely be any more severe than it was here on our floating *Finland*. Had it not been for fur coats and barrels of schnapps it would have been the end of us. Heavy mittens were also a great help. It was pitiful to see the deckhands by the rail, teeth chattering and fingers shoved under their fur coats, casting the occasional sorrowful glance towards Klippan and Masthugget with something of the same mien as Reynard the Fox looks at half a dozen plump geese that he cannot reach when he is hungry.

At last, in the evening of Christmas Day, the desired wind began to rise. Orders were issued for the institution of a strict search for ship's rats since it is a habitual abuse among the crew to conceal a number of boys around the ship unbeknown to the authorities and, once at sea, these become a burden upon the Company. It is thus not a question of four-legged rats – they are under the jurisdiction of the ship's cat – but of the two-legged variety. Three or four of them were found but to our great amazement they were wearing white stockings and skirts. *Linnaeus* makes no mention of them either in the earlier or the later edition of his System, nor have I seen them described by *Reaumur* and *Buffon*.[8] They are exactly like women, right from the crown of the head to the sole of the foot. They have eyes, ears and breasts, walk on two legs, are extremely tame and like to sleep on their backs just like other people. In London the species is well-known by the name *Ladies of Pleasure*, on the boulevards of Paris I have heard them called *Femmes d'amour*, in Swedish they are *Kärleksungar*. Our captain found them surplus to Company requirements and therefore had them transported ashore immediately in the jolly boat. To be heartily missed by many.

Chapter IV

FULL OF RHYME

Nos patriae fines, et dulcia linquimus arva – Virg.[9]

The next morning, before even the hens had woken below decks, the usual music of the sea began on the windlass and the anchor was raised. The seamen ran around like horses turning a mill and the sallies that they voiced were about as tasteful as their quids of tobacco. Day became visible and the sail was set: Farewell, Father Pilot!

Farewell to play and pastime!
The east wind's breath already fills our sails with life
And pond'rous *Finland*, riding on the raised back of the sea,
Sets sail as foam and froth before her bows do flee.
The Swedish hills now slowly dip from view
And seem no more than clouds of blackish hue
On which the sky its mighty vault doth rest.
Such sorrows occupy my Swedish breast:
I gaze at my land and watch with grieving heart
How it is stolen from my eyes as I depart.
Farewell my homeland! Of many a *Gustav* mother dear!
To many a *Karl* proud monuments you bear!
O Sweden, ancient land, your loss fills me with pain,
My heart will joyless be until I come again.
'Tis to thee, O *Atland*,[10] that I dedicate my fame,
Though Turk should offer me a Vizier's name
And a hundred thousand men to join my march on Moscow
And cap the gift with a seraglio!
However great the joy of trouncing Muscovite,
However sweet the kisses offered night by night,
A Swede I am, and Swedish e'er will be:
Forgive me, Sultan, a Viziership is not the ship for me!
And thou, who in this age holds Europe's wheel,
Controlling all by flattery and by deals -
Thou, Lord *Louis* in Paris,[11] wert thou perchance to say
'Take one of my chateaux' and bow my way,

I should return thy bow and also thy chateau
For but the smallest patch on Sweden's dear shore.
For her renown, just like her air, is manly, sound and clean,
There I first saw the light of day, there will I buried be!
Let *Hat* and *Cap* draw wide a'twain in loud disunity,[12]
An oak, whose root is shaken in the mould,
Will merely take itself a firmer hold.
When *Rome* no longer disagreed, her might began to fold,
While *England*, riven now with splits, grows free and great
For parties are the life-blood of a state.
So, whate'er may hap, may hap,
There's not a bit of me that's not a Swedish chap.

The two Swedish ships now ploughed the Kattegat. Neptune in his majestic carriage, bearing his great trident and surrounded by his playful Tritons, puts on less of a show on the water than our fullrigged sailing ships. *Finland*, like some old, big-bellied dean of Tuna with no need to hurry to a fatter living, swayed over the waves with a prudent venerable gait. *Gustav*, on the other hand, arrogant as a little secretary who has been delegated authority in some official matter, scuttled along more quickly and was out of our sight by the second day.

Chapter V

CONCERNING VOMITING, BELLBOTTOMS ETC.

Useful reading for anyone who needs to throw up. I have no motto this time, unless my noble reader is happy to put up with the following:

– – – *procumbit humi bos* – – Virg.[13]

Ugh! These young fellows are making a real disgrace of themselves! Already so drunk that they are vomiting? . . . Oh, I see,

I'm sorry! So it's really seasickness that is causing such a stink everywhere? I took it for something quite different . . .

May I be permitted to describe my poor vomiting nest? The rolling had already shaken loose the ballast in the more inexperienced of our seamen. I'll never forget the many amusing little tragedies this caused on board. My stomach was far too honourable to follow suit, which is why I'm so keen to laugh at the others.

The most manly of them stayed on deck in the fresh air and sprayed their misery over and along the side, but the weaker ones had to salvage their rebellious mesenteries in their respective cabins. In one corner lay a collapsed midshipman slowly groaning *Ulrich*[14] with his cheeks distended like two bagpipes; in the other a deckhand sat frozen with a bucket between his legs and loudly regurgitated his whole ration of peas. One poor fellow had taken his stance head to the wind at the rail so that half his dose attached itself to his fur-coat. Our unfortunate galley mate was leaving the deck with a piece of meat on his way to the galley when he had the misfortune in his haste to trip head over heels in somebody else's spew (good Swedish), at which he swore miserably and wished the devil would hammer wooden bungs into the throats of the leaky scoundrels. Then, when he tried to make up the fire under the cauldrons, the memory of the stench of vomit grew so strong in his imagination that he chundered the stove full and extinguished it to the last spark.

An even more lamentable incident afflicted our worthy hen-keeper. He was sitting in harmless silence on a chest drinking Company tea but ignorant of the fact that a sufferer was lying above him in a hammock. He was just bringing the dear and much desired cup to his thirsty lips when misfortune struck and the fellow in the hammock coughed the cup full of green bile, not omitting to spray his felt cap so that streams of slaver trickled down his face in fifteen rivulets, all of which – as if by prior agreement – flowed together into the corners of his mouth. Our unfortunate hen-king tasted the vile taste and began to vomit as heartily as the other had. He tried to swear but no more than fragments emerged: 'May – ugh – the – urr – devil – ugh – tttake you, you sw – ugh – urr – swine.' Those of us who were watching this spewy dance almost made ourselves seasick with laughter, especially since one of the seamen provided a comic epilogue. May I tell you about it? Well, Sir – but take a pinch of Havana first.

This fellow-me-lad, like the others, had not gone unmoved by the see-sawing of the ship, but NB. via the passage that is blocked when you sit down. He now stood up and observed the fate of the poor hen-keeper and it caused him to burst into such violent mirth that his cutter sprung a large leak in its after-hatch.(a) He wanted to keep it secret but his leaky, telltale bellbottoms revealed it to all eyes. Shall I tell you how it trickled? No, ugh! I pointed the swine in the direction of the heads and left, drawing from the incident the moral that a pair of bellbottoms is just as insecure a hiding place for a secret as the bosom of a woman. (b)

When I arrived in my cabin, I spared a thought for the Swedish Navy. I imagined the state it must be in when, putting to sea in haste, it is manned by a swarm of lousy peasant louts who, unused to the sea, are incapable of responding to the enemy cannon with anything apart from salvos of vomiting *ooaarrs*. My old Ovid caught my eye and provided me with a line that suits the context far better than a peasant lad aboard a ship of the line:

Apta magis Cereri, quam sunt tua corpora Marti[15]

which I would translate as follows: 'Let the seaman travel the sea and the countryman plough his field.'

How could I do other than desire that our merchant fleets should so increase in size that, when such situations arose, they were in a position to provide the Navy with trained and experienced seamen? That's what happens in England.

a) I'd almost forgotten that the third carpenter came running up just at that moment with his mallet and a little peg in his hand and full of an officious desire to caulk the leak, which increased our amusement considerably.

b) I regret this sally and would erase it were it not that it provided me with an opportunity to quote something else from Virgil. He had borrowed various witty thoughts from the unpolished verses of the poet Ennius and claimed thus to have harvested gold from dung. Why, then, should I not pluck this moral pearl from the seaman's besmirched bellbottoms?

Chapter VI

THE CONTENTS OF WHICH CAN BE SEEN BY ANYONE WHO CARES TO READ IT.

L'amour vit dans les orages – Md-e de l'Enclos[16]

The favourable wind that blew us out to sea did not favour us for long. We had scarcely had a glimpse of Shetland before a storm drove us halfway back, after which we worked our way in persistent blizzards up towards the Faroes, situated 64 degrees north.

It is not difficult to imagine what the days around New Year were like in this climate. I can assure you that the sun won't scorch the trimmings of your fur-coat if you come up here in the middle of January. We had a good deal of hard work to do just shovelling away the snow. The cold was bitter. The waterpipes in the sailors' *pantaloons* would undoubtedly have frozen up if our praiseworthy Company had not had the foresight to despatch a stock of schnapps barrels with us. I am eye-witness to the fact that many noses grew by as much as six or eight inches thanks to the icicles hanging frozen from them. Beard stubble resembled frosted juniper twigs on a sharp winter morning and the snowflakes lay on our eyebrows just as they do on window-ledges. I fib not.

Love is a hardy rogue. One might have expected him, accustomed as he is to warmer climes, to have had his fingers frozen off in winter at 64 degrees north. But I have to say, just as the amorous Frenchmen did when they were up in our chilly Lapland in 17 . . .[17]

Pour fuir l'amour
En vain on court
Jusqu'à l'astre Polaire.
Dieu! qui croiroit,
Qu'en cet endroit
On trouverait Cythere!

in Swedish:(c)

You'll not remove
The call of love
By steering to the far north,
For Venus' power
Remains in flower
Where'er you voyage forth.

To judge by what I saw here, I would imagine that the mercury never drops to freezing point in the barometer of a young man's heart. My friends had old wifie's droplets hanging from the ends of their noses but sweet Cloris still remained on their lips. They bore snowdrifts on their backs and their sweethearts in their breasts. They sang to and toasted the fair sex. So how could a Faroese winter prevail? I still remember some of the boys' ditties.

Cold winter rules this northern clime,
But summer fills my loving heart
Pierced by S – a's amorous dart.
The sun is with me all the time
As long as we two do not part.

Another

Rage, winter, as you will,
You'll never quench the flame
That, kindled by my L – a's name,
Burns bright within me still.

One of our number, whose heart love had never dared invade for fear of drowning in his throat on the way, called the others bower-bores and began to warble – –

> Venus, begone! – – Break out the drink
> And let me drain each glass.
> I'll blame the rolling of the ship
> If I fall down on my arse.

c) Translated, if I remember rightly, by Celsius.

Chapter VII

FOR THE LEARNED.

Non dubito fore plerosque – – Corn. Nepos.[18]

In order to be of some benefit in well-read circles, I feel bound to make the following observations. Since they refer to the Swedish language, they may serve as an appendix to Principal Secretary Ihre's dictionary.[19] Seamen are great abusers of language.

The whole world knows what it means *to have a dram*, but here aboard ship they talk instead of having a *Nisse* or a *Lasse*; the former refers to a 1/4 gill of schnapps and the latter to 1/2 a gill. Here we are not allowed to eat *food* like other people, we have to have *victuals*. To *purra* someone on shore means to play a trick on them but here it means to open a door, grab hold of someone's foot and say "it's seven bells" – which, in its turn, is supposed to define what time it is. The action of throwing out over the stern a triangular board attached to a line from which red rags hang at intervals is called, in a phrase, *heaving the log*. A square cabin goes by the name of the *roundhouse*, which utterly conflicts with Euclid, who proves that a round square is an impossibility. Similarly, they have a magical device with sundry pieces of glass screwed to it with which they are able to read the sun without pointing their eyes in its direction; it works by bewitching the sun down from the heights onto the rim of the water itself, in which position it looks rather like a red felt cap.

This thingummy doesn't have any more than three corners but nevertheless has to be called an *ottkant* or *octant.* Yet another poke in the eye for Maths! *Knop* is a rude word ashore that ladies, anyway, would never allow past their lips, but it is used daily by sailors and denotes an English mile; they say, for example, that the *Prins* makes 9 *knop* an hour whereas *Finland* only makes 8. There is a great deal of talk here of *bosun's meat, constable's meat, carpenter's meat*[20] and the like, and in the beginning I thought they were talking about salted meat or stockfish. But when I saw that these were all real people, I suspected the bosun, the carpenter and all the rest of those who could have *meat* added to the ends of their names of being anthropophagous. As a result, at first, I could hardly stop myself scowling at them and recalling that great man-eater *Polyphemus* who, so Homer tells us, devoured all of Ulysses' travelling companions while graciously promising to eat the hero himself last of all. If they are capable of eating other people, I thought, my turn will certainly come, and I couldn't even pass them on deck without a secret shudder until I finally noticed that they no more devoured Christian flesh than other good people did. For, aboard ship, *meat* at the end of a word means the same as *vice* at the beginning of a word on shore. Were I to use seaman's language at home, I would convert the Vice District Judge into the District Judge's Meat, the Vice Mayor to the Mayor's Meat and the Vice Pastor to the Holy Old Man's Meat and so on. Those little round *et ceteras* that are collected up after sheep and cattle are referred to as plums here, which is why Plum-digger is the exact equivalent of *dairymaid.* Quartermaster M – – said to the sailors a few days ago: *Right, boys, haul in time to my singing.* At which he set up a *hoa, hoa, ho-ing* that in normal Swedish might be called *bellowing* but certainly not *singing.* A *monkey* as any peasant in Östergylln knows is a hairy creature with four legs; here, however, it is the nickname of a little sail. The nightwatch from 1 o'clock to 4 is named the *dogwatch,* but woe betide any newcomer who takes it literally for he is likely to learn, at some cost to his shoulders, that seafolk as often as not say one thing and mean another. *Dagg*[21] – now isn't that a blessed gift from God ashore, especially during a long drought? Here, however, it is the most wretched thing on the whole vessel, the most terrible rope's end among all the rope-work: ask any ordinary seaman. *Smelling caskets*, those nice articles that are of such service to the fair sex when they suffer from aristocratic little swoons or a touch of French faintness, have been treated with a complete lack of respect here. I have heard the phrase applied to a pair of tarry bellbottoms (d), however small the resemblance may be either in terms of smell or of style. Not to mention the enormous difference there is between a lady's nose and a sailor's aftercastle.(e)

These and many more corrupt turns of phrase occur at sea and I find it all the more painful that, to all appearances, the same ill-usage seems to be taking root on land. Many a time, and with sadness, have I heard such expressions as *to haul in a girl*, *to hook a skirt*, *to brace*, *to board* and others.

d) The reason being the unpleasant atmosphere that forces its way out of them, especially when the sailors are standing at the wheel.

e) A nice expression that I have borrowed from Dean Lenaeus' *Delsboa Illustrata.*[22]

Chapter VIII

Subsequitur clamorque virum stridorque rudentum. Virg.[23]

We were now in the month of January 1770 and had managed to get past the top of the land of the Scots. The huge swell was beginning to subside somewhat. Intending to take advantage of the calm I went down to my cabin where I hacked a hole in the ice in my frozen ink-pot and took pen in hand. But, oh, the faithless sea!

I write – whoops, I'm falling! Biörkman (f) help me back!
Ouch! Ouch! I took a devil of a crack!
What's wrong? A storm, alas! The cabin stands on end,
Desk, books, glass and me slide from end to end.
Pandemonium rages through my little den,
    Fifteen rivulets of ink
    round my fingers flow and link,
Drowning every rhyme before it leaves the pen.
Quick, Biörkman, batten the hatch, that's some sea out there!
Terrified and cold and wet, I make for the open air.
Out of the road, Ship's Scribbler! Now she starts to cant,
So together we skite sideways using the seat of our pants.
Oh God! screams the Scribbler, the ship's beginning to crack,
And together on the seat of our pants we skite right back.
Two legs are insufficient to help out in a gale,
I reach the deck eventually on my belly like a snail.
Our Captain's voice was bellowing 'Get down those sails!'
The crew were toiling on the deck pulling at shrouds and yards.
They blistered skin with hauling, hawsers ripped their nails,
And ropes like whips about their heads cracked close and hard.
High in the rigging like gunfire the flying sheets were rent,
Below the deck the whining pumps their fearsome message sent.
Each wave that thundered o'er us revealed a dreadful crypt,
A suffocating watery grave for Captain, crew and ship.
Our faces like the air around revealed all fear and dread
As Storm's barbarian progeny from far and wide drew nigh
To foam beneath us in the waves and fill the air above our heads
With white and flying spume that crashed against the very sky.

A fearful black cloud brings omens of the terrors of the night,
The rudder's gone, our wave-smashed ship no longer watertight.
Her beams are groaning, planks shattered in the deck,
And *Finland* now is tossed by wind and wave, a wreck.

The storm described here dogged us for a full 24 hours and it was all the more dangerous since it was blowing us straight back towards the cliffs of Scotland. In the evening we went on our knees and recited the storm-prayers and orders were given that not an eye should be shut that night. The carpenters were standing ready to use their axes on the masts, the spars were threatening the whole time to crash down on our heads, and it was enough of a task just to keep ourselves positioned wherever we happened to be.

The weather eased a little around noon the following day but only to gain renewed strength. The elements seemed to have joined in a conspiracy against us. For a good six weeks we should have considered a moderate gale a stroke of luck, we were so used to severe gales. If I had kept a diary of this unprecedented sailing backwards and forwards, it could not have looked other than as follows:

Monday - - storm
Tuesday - - storm
Wednesday - - ditto
Thursday - - ditto, and so on every day of the week and right until the middle of February when the winds, though now less violent, still continued to blow head on to our bows. We were fated to a series of surprise attacks by all the terrors of nature in these latitudes for, while the sea persecuted us with storms, hurricanes and violent currents, the sky above our heads threatened us with blood-red auroras and silent lightning, not to mention the long, dark and frosty winter nights. To describe it all would take an eternity, but one hurricane (my hand is still trembling with terror) one hurricane, which we endured on the 24th Jan., left impressions on the ship and on our hearts far too deep to be forgotten.

(f) The author's servant

Chapter IX

CONCERNING THE DREADFUL DESTRUCTION OF JERUSALEM [24]

Monstrum horrendum, informe, ingen - - - Virg.[25]

Hurricane! What a dread apparition! The vilest spectacle mortal eye can behold, next only to the slaughter left on the field of war by some bloody victor. How can I depict you so that others may see? Art has not yet mixed colours vile enough to paint your image but, since you once terrified the life out of me, I must take what vengeance I am capable of. If I am spared, landlubbers will be told what an arrogant tyrant you are at sea!

It began in the morning with a strong wind that steadily increased right through to evening. The sails were furled tight. Spars and yards were removed. Thrice the monkey-gaff was fixed and thrice it was torn to shreds. I shall not attempt to describe the doom-laden horizon, the screaming winds or the murderous mountains of water that attacked our sides like battering rams and threw us up and down in turn, for they surpass all imagination. But I am malicious enough to wish that a dozen or so of our prosperous powder-puff heroes from home had been here for no more than three or four minutes – the poor souls would never have survived a whole day of it. I am certain, however, that it would have made them ponder upon their mortality rather than upon their well-curled locks and, at the very least, they wouldn't have dared continue maintaining that *Voltaire* has a better religion than *Luther*. There were times when *Finland* was so buried between sky-high waves that the sky above my head was a patch no bigger than one of those stiff skirts that used to be everyday wear. This gave me a far better understanding than ever before of my beloved Naso when he writes:

– totidemque videntur,
Quot veniunt fluctus, ruere atque irrumpere montes.[26]

The approach of the darkness of night increased our terror. We balanced our way to table and got a little food into our stomachs and a great deal on our clothes. It could almost have been argued that the roast chickens we had in front of us were alive since they showed every inclination to fly from windward to leeward the whole time. With the usual storm prayers we commended ourselves into the hands of the Almighty and, silently awaiting the result, left the ship to the wind and waves.

The clock strikes ten! Out of the way, out of the way! *A lump of water*! A mortally terrifying apparition, about as high as Otterhällan and as wide as Hisingen,[27] suddenly crashed in over the bows, hurled a huge anchor onto the deck, shattered the rail and the shroud-boards, dragged spars, jolly boat and launch across the deck with it in spite of their double lashings, raged towards the stern overturning everything in its way, doused the lights by the compasses and swept a whole huddle of sailors who had crowded together in the roundhouse passage right back to the crescent rail of the quarterdeck. Our vigilant grey-haired captain himself was left swimming back and forth on the deck and had it not been for the end of a rope that fortune blessed by putting it within his reach both *Finland* and Mrs Ekeberg would have been grieving widows. The second and fourth mates, the doctor and others who were sitting at a table under the sundeck were thrown head over heels across that table and backwards into the gangway, where they swam around for some minutes among seamen and benches thinking that they were already at the bottom of the sea. What, apart from Our Lord's net, could have rescued these fish? All the more so as the sea had knocked out the hatches on the side where they were floating. Just how little was left above the surface is shown by the fact that the supercargo, the assistants and myself were wading around in the roundhouse up to our shins in water. Between decks, the sea rushed down the companionway with a speed that can only be compared to Trollhättan Falls,[28] smashed the door to the ship's secretary's cabin and left a little lake in every corner. Even when I went down to my little study two hours later, I discovered my bedclothes to be three hundredweight heavier than usual. *Schenberg's* great lexicon[29] was floating on the floor like a dredging-barge, my red slippers were sailing behind it like a couple of herring boats and, worse still, my poor wig-box, also there among the shipping, had sprung a leak and had its whole cargo ruined. Oh, why didn't I have it insured in Hamburg?

The events are far too serious, you might say, to be described with a smile on the lips. All right, I agree. But who is to say that there isn't some delight in danger once it is over and done with? Apart from which, given the scale of confusion aboard a ship that is home to 150 people, there are bound to be some amusing scenes among the tragic ones. There is one poor devil lying there with a broken pipe in his hand and damning and blasting for all he is worth. Over there is someone else, tankard to mouth as he rolls head over heels to the far side. A third is praying, a fourth looking for his cap. One chap is crying over his crushed arm, another over his crushed punch-bowl. A couple of fellows are riding on a sofa that is sliding from rail to rail, and the rest are swimming round the deck like so many large skate.

There was, however, no one aboard *Finland* who did not think she was going to the bottom for, while the ship was underwater, there were three truly dreadful crashes just as if she had run onto a cliff, and we judged from this buffeting that she was bound to break into three. Wherever you looked you saw nothing but living corpses until our captain had succeeded in shaking the ocean out of himself and told us that the danger was already over – a statement that inspired as much joy as the lump of water had inspired terror. I cannot say what colour my face was but I do remember that my pulse was going like that of a lover caught and cudgelled in the bed of another man's wife. But there is no cowardice in that, for Death is grim when his jaws open in the deep. Even the fearless *Carl*, who smiled at Death when it came rushing from the mouth of a thundering cannon, turned pale when the waves foamed over his boat during his crossing to Ystad from the bombardment of Stralsund.[30]

The creaking of the pumps kept sleep from our eyes all night but our blessed vessel held her own against the enraged waves and still bore us all in her faithful bosom. She had a list, however, and when we investigated below decks we found that the cannon had broken loose. The glassware on board had suffered considerable damage and all of our china was in pieces. Our first mate was confined to bed because of a fall he had taken in the confusion. The steward had broken his arm and Quartermaster M – , with just as much pain, had suffered the loss of a cask of schnapps. Some of the crew claimed to have been washed overboard when the sea surged over us and then thrown back on deck as the water poured out, which sounds even more unlikely than the look-out's insistence that the water had reached right up to him in the foretop.

A glimpse of daylight was now beginning to show up in the sky, accompanied by joy on our faces. I had never spent a more wretched night and thus I had never seen a more delightful morn. Hope was rekindled in our breasts. Like the Trojans who, after the departure of the Greeks, viewed with joy the fields in which their heroes had perished beneath the enemy blades, we walked with pleasure round our battlefield and collected up the caps, gloves and wigs that our departing watery foe had left behind. Though the rudder was damaged and there were cracks here and there in the deck, we could only rejoice at our own salvation.

A sermon of thanksgiving was delivered the following Sunday, its text being Matthew 8: 'Jesus slept in the ship as the storm raged.' After that a respectable sum was collected for a widow and her three small children, her sailor husband having been hurled down into the sea from the foremast during the inclement weather.

Chapter X

UNLIKE ALL THOSE THAT PRECEDE IT.

– – *nutu tremefecit Olympum* – [31]

All of these lengthy and threatening adversities I have described had, in no small measure, given us long faces: like the air, they were now bleak and sharp. It was, however, impossible to do other than see the hand of *God* particularly in this most recent event. Huge and ponderous objects, lashed down with double ropes, had been hurled overboard and yet, out of fifty people who had been walking free and unroped on the deck, not one was missing. Was that not a manifest miracle? This perception inspired my soul anew with thoughts of the *Lord on High*, who built heaven as his throne and the earth as his footstool.[32] I let my joyful emotion express itself in the so-called hexameters that follow. My Muse might just once do me a worthwhile service.

Earnest now, my Muse. Fall silent, playful tones of habit!
Hallowed be my song for I address my *Lord* and *Master*
And with trembling mortal lips approach eternal wonders.

Rise, my savéd soul and borrow the wings of the eagle,
Fly 'mongst the starry hosts to the purity of the heavens,
Seek the throne upon which the eternal Thunderer rules,
Peerless in His majesty, encircled by a myriad suns,
Giving all things life, worshipped by worlds uncountable,
Feared by the demons of hell, praised by the children of heaven.

Cast yourself down in adoration and give thanks to your Lord.
Speak to your God, your face cloaked in the mask of atonement
For your mortal eyes cannot endure the power of His gaze.
Speak for us and say: Lord, look down upon the spheres below
And see upon the endless ocean, on the home of the whale,
Where drifts a frail bark clutching its sighing crew to its bosom,
Tossed among the towering breakers of the storm-torn waters.

O Lord, Thou who ridest the heavens in the clouds' thundery
chariot,
Command from Thy secret fastness the far roaring tempest,
Breathe aside buttressed clouds, extinguish the flame of Thy lightning;
O terrible God! lay aside Thine avenging arrows
And have mercy, for Thy name through the ages is Father.
Look in Thine ineffable tenderness upon the *Finland*,
Turn not Thine eyes from us, for Thy smile, O mighty Father,
Is life to all creatures, as Thy rage is the end of creation.

Lord, Thou hast shown Thine arm and our hair has risen in terror,
Caused the frosty darkness of night to consume the light of day,
Whipped the deep to foam, hurled flames from the angry heavens;
The storm trumpets of death have heralded our chastisement
And we saw our graves. But Thine ever-merciful goodness
Hearkened unto our cries and Thou rebuked the defiant waves.

Almighty God, seen in all things and understood by no one,
No mortal eye can pierce Thy holy mysteries,
Yet may an honest sigh or prayer reach unto Thine ear,
And we thank Thee.

Hallowed be Thy name, O Thou eternal king of heaven.
Praise Him, ye heavenly hosts; honour Him, ye living creatures!
Our saviour in our distress. Ye oceans acknowledge His might!
Sing of your *Creator's* mercy, O ye birds of the air!
And you, mankind whom He has saved, honour your Almighty
Father.

Chapter XI

WHICH DESERVES TO BE READ BECAUSE IT IS SO SHORT.

Navita de ventis, de tauris narrat arator – N.N.[33]

Stern lords do not rule for long, so it is said. We hoped that the westerly storms would now cease after having put all their combined strength into this most recent one. In vain. To our misfortune, the winds, which by their very nature are inconstant, were now all too constant. Whenever we had the winds of the air in our favour, we had treacherous currents against us in the water. Our oldest seaman proclaimed that he had never been so ill-favoured. Strange things happen on the main, to be sure but that a ship as well-equipped and wisely mastered as our *Finland* should be swept back almost from the Bay of Biscay all the way to Norway must be one of those events that occur only once in a thousand years.

I have, however, remarked that there is nothing so bad that it does not bring a little good in its train. These storms provided the crew with many an extra *Lasse* to stouten their hearts for, as soon as the storms began to whine in the rigging, the schnapps bell rang on deck. From the happy faces of the crew it was easy to see that the dreadful bass-notes of the former frightened them less than the sweet descant of the latter delighted them.

Anyone who sees East Indiamen in the first fortnight after their homecoming is likely to take them for disorderly louts because, as long as the celebration lasts, a good many red cloaks will be forced to step into the gutter to make way for a staggering Nankin jacket. I remember myself how often I have been elbowed out of the road by them in Masthugget. At sea, however, they are as gentle as lambs and, what may seem even more unlikely, they are actually God-fearing. I can't give you the reason, though the fact that the knout exists aboard ship and that there are neither skirts nor inn-signs probably has a good deal to do with it. And the storms that occur at sea now and again probably also contribute. I heard our captain say on one occasion: *Qui nescit orare, discat navigare.*[34]

Chapter XII

A COMPARISON BETWEEN THE TOWN OF KUNGSBACKA AND THE SHIP FINLAND.

Humano capiti cervicem pictor equinam
Jungere si velit – – – Horat.[35]

Homer compares his bold Achilles to a fly;[36] Holberg, with even less reason, places Christian IV on a par with our Gustavus Adolphus.[37] A Dutch skipper compared his sweetheart's nose to the rudder of his ship, and a priest in Norway said that man is like a fur rug – full of vermin. 'My children', he called from the pulpit, 'man is like a hairy skin full of lice and nits. He can scratch the lice off but not the nits, for they are thoroughly attached to the tangled hair. You can likewise get rid of the sins that you commit (g) but you will never be free of original sin.'

If a comparison such as that can win approval I have no doubt that mine is worthy of admiration. The affinity between the Royal Port and Burgh of Kungsbacka[38] and the Swed. East Ind. Co. ship *Finland* at least has the advantage of being far more obvious.

There is plenty of cattle there, just as there is here. There are two long parallel streets in Kungsbacka and we have the same on *Finland*, namely Larboard Street and Starboard Street. They reckon they have many side-streets but we can boast of Smith's Lane, Ropemaker Row, Bosun's Walk and as many more as are needed by our special workshops. They may outdo us in the number of taverns but we outdo them in the art of drinking. Our roundhouse corresponds to their Town-house, just as our mizzen-mast can without shame be compared to their church steeple, both being wooden and painted red. There is always a heap of old timbers and boards to be seen lying on the square in Kungsbacka, and on the fences around the young women hang out their shifts to dry; we have the same sight here up on the foredeck, if I may be permitted to compare sailors' linen with that of the aforementioned. There is scarcely any great difference in quality, but I fear that it is uncouth of me to examine young ladies' nether-regions so closely and even more so to speak of them, so I shall say no more on the topic – – They have a pillory there, we have the main-mast here; who--s are whipped at the former, seamen are flogged at the latter. One occurs according to the laws of the land, the other according to the Ship's Articles. The majority of the inhabitants there are poor and go barefoot in the summer; the greater part of the crew of *Finland* don't own more than a smock and wear nothing but their natural shoes when it is warm. I saw a hunch-backed tailor in Kungsbacka and we have a similar little camel here too. When nature calls in Kungsbacka they go around a corner; our Finlanders lay their eggs at the heads. Whereas a gale may deprive us of our topsail, they can be deprived of their trading charter by a storm in Parliament. In short, with the exception of the clogs that I've heard clattering on the streets there but haven't heard in our community, it should be clear to anyone with eyes in his head that the Swed. East Ind. ship *Finland* resembles the Port and Burgh of Kungsbacka very closely and, were both put under the hammer at an auction, I fear that the selling price of the latter would be a couple of barrels of gold fewer.

g) Sins of commission.

Chapter XIII

WITH WHICH I EXPECT TO EARN THE FRIENDSHIP OF THE FAIR SEX, A CUDGELLING FROM OFFICERS, AND POWDER THROWN IN MY FACE BY DANDIES.

– – *nescis quid faemina possit* – Ovid.[39]

I shall begin with our crossing of the ocean. On the morning of the 7th Feb. we were amazed to see the cliffs of Shetland to port. We had reason to believe that we were nearer to the Bay of Biscay than to them and thus, at first, we took them for a stationary cloud but as daylight increased the truth was revealed. This, more than anything, demonstrates the peril into which a sailing vessel can be brought by currents. It was decided that it was inadvisable to continue struggling against the elements. The relevant gentlemen took into account the facts that the ship was now without boats and that provisions might run short were we to have a slow voyage to the port of destination, which was the Cape. Since the one was considered to be as essential to the ship as the other was to our stomachs, it was decided to seek for some safe haven and, in the circumstances, Norway was the most conveniently situated.

Once we had turned our noses towards the North Pole again I became thoroughly indignant at the thought that we had suffered so badly for no less than two months to no purpose at all, all the more so as these wretched northern waters would soon have to be ploughed through yet again. In my vexation, I called a fool whoever it was who first built a ship and was arrogant enough to raise a sail on the stormy deep. I recalled wise old Cato, who had made up his mind on three things: never to confide a secret to a woman, never to go to bed at night without having done a good deed and, lastly, never to travel by sea when he could get to his destination by land. I sought for any reason why mankind, which nature has provided with feet for walking but not fins for swimming, should have the courage to sit down on a few planks nailed together and float in mortal danger across the realm of the fish to the other side of the globe. Money, money, was what first came to my mind, but then I asked myself why that should be so desirable? And lo! my heart answered me on behalf of all seafarers that a sweetheart, a little well-constructed idol five feet tall with a fiery pair of eyes and rosy lips and a bosom breathing love and a neat ankle and – – – Alas! Oh! Alack! – – In short, a pretty girl is the spring that really drives the works, whatever the ends may be. For whom if not for Chloris do we poor lads slave? A little friend, little missy, little pretty-eyes is and always will be at the centre of our considerations. No ship would ever have been wrecked at sea if our eyes had not first encountered the treacherous hidden cliffs that are concealed among the billows of the swelling bosom of a beauty. Our desires may make as many detours as they like but they will eventually all flow together in the bridal bed just as naturally as rivers rush to the sea. Why did Greece sail to distant Troy? – For *Helen*. Who lent wings to the great *Gustavus Adolphus* when he flew in twenty-four hours from the army in Kalmar all the way to Stockholm? Love and *Ebba Brahe*.[40] Why did mighty *Hercules* risk his life in so many bloody and perilous ventures? To please his pretty *Deianira*, of course. What was it that inspired the Russians to fight so boldly at Khotin in 1769? Honour, perhaps? No! Turkish silver-belts, perhaps? Not that, either! The Grand Vizier's harem, then? Oh, yes! The whole world would put up with a scratch or two for that. *Omnia vincit amor*, as the preacher Ovid says.[41]

So why are we travelling to the Indies? The answer is there to be read in the eyes of Swedish womanhood. We would run around the whole earth for one meaningful look from a beautiful girl. We would sail far away from them so as to get that much closer to them at the same time. Who would dare go on a ship where death sits on the rails all around were it not for such a precious reward? Thinking of pretty girls and becoming a poet is one and the same thing. I can already feel my vein of verse opening – let it run down the paper – ding – dong.

O maids of royal Sweden, ye tyrants left at home,
Worthy of adoration, bright torches of the North,
Who stay behind in comfort while we do venture forth,
 'Tis for you we voyage east across the foam,
 For you, you wicked, pretty little beasts!
That you may sweetly lap at tea and gossip,
We brave the waves aboard a storm-tossed ship;
To bring home porcelain for your trifling pleasure,
 We face the winds and stormy weather.
 We run the risk of drowning
That you may grace the ball, clad in China's all, unfrowning.
Where you will meet some dandy, a coiffured jimmy,
 For whom sweet Lisa's shimmy
Is the sail he wants to raise. For he's never been to sea
And thinks that ships are chauffeur-driven gigs
That parade the Allée full of powdered wigs
 Like his – along o' you, unfaithful maid -
Squand'ring every hard-earned cent we made.
 Or an officer, albeit threadbare,
Who nicked his lackey's flour to sprinkle in his hair,
Whose petty arrogance rests on his noble birth
Though tavern habits long since drowned ancestral worth.
 An epauletted poltroon
 – Under fire, ever brave! -
But he's the kind to conquer in your less than constant bower
Though his coat was bought on credit that we gave.
Thus sheep are fleeced to warm the shoulders of another
And drones consume the food their worker fellows gather.
Oh, girls, for shame! Fall not a victim of these idlers deceit,
A seaman may not bow and scrape but he picks up the receipt.
Your dandy does his courting with sycophantic verses

While we support our pleadings with overflowing purses.
Your officer may offer you a withered family tree,
But with a pocket full of doubloons we can woo financially.
Oh, girls! Reward our toil and ardour:
How can your dandy's barbered locks
Compare with flowers, silks and rocks!
And ancestors won't fill your larder,
So let old Epaulettes be banished
With his, not your, escutcheon tarnished.
Then come and join us as we prance
To the clinking music of the doubloon dance,
To the clinking music of the doubloon dance.

Chapter XIV

OUR ARRIVAL IN NORWAY.

– – – *Trojae sic fata ferebant* – [42]

The date was now the 10th Feb. 1770. There had been a time when I thought it more likely that the heavens would fall than that we should see the cliffs of Norway at that date. But it was written in the stars and, thus, it was our fate to be freezing here at just the time we had expected to be baking in the sun below the line. Who would have believed at home that, after two months voyaging in a ship capable of carrying 32 sails simultaneously, we should not have managed to get farther than a day's journey from Gothenburg?

Nature, as if to correct the disorder caused by the troubled North Sea, has built safe harbours all over the Norwegian archipelago and, moreover, has populated its shores with a rough-hewn breed among which are to be found the finest pilots in the world. Our purser had scarcely announced our presence with a thunderous salvo before four or five small boats came creeping out from among the rocks. The mist was quite thick but they smelled the powder and smoke and arrived aboard without difficulty – Fine Day! – Good-day, dear fellow!

The Norskie we got as a guide was tall to the point of towering, a giant with a nose that would recommend him as a suitor to those women who have some understanding of physical proportions. It stood out like a bow and took up at least a third of his face. The pipe that succeeded the quids of tobacco in the corner of his mouth didn't manage to project beyond the point of that nose and seemed to be provided as some sort of smoky altar for it. It showed all the marks of the climate, being red and inured to cold like his other limbs. He was a resolute man and commanded the rudder with a certainty that revealed that he was familiar with every rock in the passage. By 4 o'clock in the afternoon he had brought us into Svinörsund[43] where our exhausted *Finland* anchored, by now resembling a woman who, struck by a storm during a pleasure trip on the water, had mislaid her gloves, lost her hair-ribbons and torn her lace cuffs before finally reaching the safety of shore with her hair down and tears in her eyes.

Precious Norway! Last hiding place of the oppressed as well as of swindlers! How shall I begin to describe you? The comparison with the terrifying deep made you a paradise in our eyes. Your bare mountains changed into pleasure-gardens, your fishermen's huts into palaces and your ragged daughters into princesses of wondrous beauty. The sea had had the same effect on us as novels had on the Knight of La Mancha,[44] whose imagination created royal palaces out of inns and giants out of windmills. When he embraced the filthy Maritornes, who still stank of the stable boy and the cowshed, he thought he was holding a princess of angelic beauty in his arms and that her fine clothes were all scented with ambergris and precious incenses. The same happy enchantment possessed our young men as they went ashore.

Chapter XV

OUR STAY IN SVINÖRSUND.

Nos convivia, nos praelia virginum Cantamus – – Horat.[45]

Our supercargo and our captain began immediately to deal with the urgent concerns and improvements of the ship. They had set up their headquarters at the house of a shipping registrar by the name of Galtrup, a well-travelled and cheerful old man who had seen every demon in creation including the devil himself and his closest kin, that is, the Holy Fathers of the Inquisition in Spain and Portugal. He entertained his guests with stories and roast crow, which he called a *fine gamebird*. The former were pleasing to the ear for the old man had a pleasant smile and was able to spin out the yard remnant of a story to a full furlong. The latter, however, was not so pleasing to the taste. Which is why the gentlemen were compelled to bring in the officers' cook to supervise the registrar's cook. Mr Galtrup himself – as well as his son-in-law Ferrö, round as a beer-barrel and a skipper by trade – both found our Swedish food very respectable and proved it by their all-devouring appetites.

The others, meanwhile, scurried around all the neighbouring villages, taking guns, fiddles and wine bottles with them. Mornings were spent hunting in the ravines. Von Heland, our assistant supercargo, kept us in game the whole time. We were eating duck and wild goose while roast crow was being served up at the registrar's. Among other things, he brought down a huge eagle (Oh that it were the Russian eagle!) that had been sitting high up on a cliff. It plunged down the precipice but still seemed ready to defend itself, at which there followed a lively hand-to-hand combat between the two parties until the wounded beast finally bit the dust from a blow from the marksman's gunstock. I got his quill feathers to write this chapter with and our ingenious fourth mate has since made a pair of splendid candlesticks from the two feet.

During the afternoons we stormed the farmhouses and wherever we went there was a party. The lasses were dragged away from their spinning wheels to join in reels and they were only too willing to help us shake the scurvy out of our joints. Each and every one of us gained a *dame de ses pensées*.[46] We played hide-and-seek and danced ring-dances such as Changing Spouses and Adam Had Seven Sons. When our captain heard this, he shrugged his shoulders and said:

'When the devil is hungry, he'll eat muck.' A withering comment but true to the last letter – though no impropriety occurred for our ship's pastor was with us and threatened us with having to do public penance in church. May I be permitted to describe our Norwegian goddesses? *Cui bono?*[47] one might interject, but, my gracious reader, don't interrupt my flow with such a tedious question: all-too-few of my chapters could survive it, and think of the innumerable host of folios that would be discarded from our collections if we were to gauge them by that measure. So don't bother me with your *cui bono?*, I beg you for once and for all – – So, step forward then, my pretty ones! Little Gunilla, Big Gunilla, Martha, Åsele, Agnill! I shall depict you in as few words as possible.

Little Gunilla, all our eyes were raised to you! A sweet-nosed, brown-eyed child with black extremities, 4 foot 5 inches tall and equally wide – as long as we were there, at least. If she has filled out in any direction since, that's her business. *Big Gunilla* was a two and a half hundredweight barrel of flesh on two legs supported by two feet that seemed to swallow the floorboards she walked on. Anyone wanting to track her down could never go astray for, wherever she put her foot down in a snow-drift, it left a mark two feet square. *Åsele*, whose two squinting eyes bestowed captivating glances on several people at the same time, almost brought the boys to blows since all of them desired to receive most rays of that inconstant light. *Martha's* splendour was her two beautiful hands: the right hand had no equal except the left, which in turn could only be compared to a dung-fork. Lovable hands! Kiss them if you want to! – – *Agnill*, on the other hand, was a nice little piece whom it was impossible to look at without feeling indignant about that wretched *not* in the sixth commandment. She was pretty, well-contoured, chatty, sixteen years old and quick; in short, the only thing she lacked in order to possess all the qualities of a well brought-up girl was a touch of lust. But in that respect she was a true farmgirl. Ugh, country girls! Nor were the others any better. The language of pieces of eight, so thoroughly understood in Cadiz as well as in Masthugget, was wasted here just as unprofitably as the language of the eyes. The wintry nature of the country had extended right into their hearts. They were so stupid, they had no grasp of things, they didn't want to – – What a shame that they hadn't learnt a little urbanity!

Have no fear, then, you Swedish maidens we left behind! Those of you who think you have rights to some of the hearts aboard *Finland*! I can tell you in confidence that the lads made no conquests here and, if they meet similarly unaccommodating Gunillas at the Cape and in Canton, they will never be unfaithful to you.

In connection, so to speak, with the foregoing I should like to append here the following account of the wedding of three couples that we had the opportunity of witnessing in Spangereid church on Sunday, the 18th of February. The wedding party processed in slowly pair by pair in three columns. Apart from the dear creatures already described, the throng was adorned by the presence of the worthy Mrs Ferrö who sailed majestically in wearing a floor-length calico dress and surrounded by the most beautiful maidens of the parish. An attentive imagination portrayed her to my eyes as Dido and her nymphs, and the chilly granite walls naturally made me think of her cool grotto. We young Swedes, who had drawn ourselves up in line at the sides, puffed out the frills on our chests and arranged our double-chins in the hope of receiving a glance from the Dido of Svinör as she approached. She actually did move her eyes graciously in our direction but it was difficult to judge who was the lucky one as her eyes never alighted where they were aimed since, in that respect, our heroine resembled the Åsele I have already referred to. While the priest was reading I thought that her eyes were directed at Heaven but I have since worked out that it was me she was looking at.

Now for the bridal couples. The first was a young lad with a lass of the same age. The lad stepped forward with a look of triumph but the maid had a tear in her eye – probably out of sympathy for any onlooker who might imagine she was bringing her maidenhead to the bridal bed. The second couple seemed to be a widower and a twenty-year-old girl, but the third was something quite different. There, in full finery, was an ugly old biddy who had the furrows of a centenarian on her face and who could certainly count ten autumns since she lost her final tooth. A trembling head swayed on her long shrivelled neck and her upper cheeks were equipped with two lumps that stood out like twin bastions guarding her sunken eyes. In a word, a spectre that ought never to have approached a churchyard except to be gathered in to her ancestors, and here she was with an eighteen-year-old lad at her side and was to be joined to him by the bonds of love. When the priest pronounced over them the words 'May they be blessed with fruit and offspring,' there was general amusement along the pews. But I put my hat in front of my face and wept for my heart told me that it deserved no more than tears. The poor bridegroom, tied to his old and all-too-durable hulk, seemed to me to be in the same situation as those Christian martyrs of whom it is told that they were lashed fast to half-rotted corpses in order to be slowly tortured to death by the stench and the cold. Unhappy the man who takes a troll for her gold! Praise be to Providence that I don't love antiques!

The ridiculousness of such marriages is too utterly obvious to need mentioning. Why doesn't the law count them as bestiality? I conclude with two lines by Nicander:[48]

> Beatings await old wives who take unshaven lads,
> Cuckolding awaits old men who take inconstant lasses.

p.s.

During the sermon a number of small children had begun to make a noise, which made our zealous preacher pound his hand on the pulpit and say: *Children, if you want to talk, I shall keep quiet.* That suggestion followed us aboard, along with the priest himself, who came to dinner on the ship.

Chapter XVI

WHICH IS THE NEXT AFTER THE FOREGOING.

Laudat mercator, quas vult extrudere merces – N.N.[49]

During this period there was a market aboard ship every day. The neighbouring villages brought the delicacies of the country on board every morning. The seamen bought endless quantities of rough spirits and bitter beer, and the midshipmen drank so much milk that we eventually called them *the noble sons of Madame* Ox, that is, calves. Fishing boats surrounded the ship like goslings around a grown goose and the closest of the mountains were whitewashed with shirts, sheets and half-sleeves that the women of the district had washed for the crew. Ferrö, in particular, plied a lucrative trade with the *Finland*. He was prepared to offer us anything except his *pretty wife*. Sugar, syrup, oxen, sheep, dogs, schnapps, mittens – everything was for sale. I shan't easily forget how he soiled the benches under the shade deck with his firkins of syrup, nor the eloquence with which he lured gleaming pieces of eight his way – – It was his pleasure to serve the Swedes; he considered them his most worthy compatriots. But the Jutlanders, ugh! They were rogues from head to foot – – – We could be quite confident that he was only trying to be of service to us, not to skin us – – His wares were good – The Jutlanders wouldn't get them at such a favourable price but the Swedes are our brothers – –

We remained lying here for three weeks, a golden age for the whole neighbourhood given the iron-age oppression they live in. The pieces of eight we left behind will have enabled them to avoid the sheriff's distraints for this year at least. Rocky Norway is a haven for foreign refugees but a house of bondage for her own native children.[50] They are oppressed by taxes and it is rare for a Norwegian to advance to any position of importance in his homeland. The mighty drink the tears of the common people from golden goblets, as an unknown author has put it. I couldn't hear their sighs without blessing the star that allowed me to be born a son of freedom in old Sweden.

Slavish by mentality,
From childhood ever used to fetters,
Bowing low before their betters,
Norway's progeny!

Humankind's esteemed prize,
Freedom, mother of all good,
Cannot be honoured as she should
When clad in autocratic guise.

Raise your voices in debate,
Fathers of this downpressed folk!
Speak out! Cast off the silent yoke!
Dissent's the life-blood of a state.

The Swedish farmer lives there free
While you are ranked below your cattle.
Few coppers in your pockets rattle
Once the sheriff's been.

Brother Norway! Why not come
Into the Swedish fold? When all is said,
The Danish king can have instead
Our Pomeranian scum.[51]

Then you would see a real nation,
Upright and mighty in freedom's dawn,
Of all the laws of slavery shorn,
Trusting in its own salvation.

Freedom to speak and freedom to write -
This is the armour that we wear.[52]
No secret enemy would dare
To meddle with such might.

But I see that I am straying too far from the goal that my motto seems to suggest. This is not the first time this has happened to me, nor is it likely to be the last. For why should I follow rules when what I am writing about has none? The following piece has to be squeezed in here even if I have to use a screw-press to do it. The episode is peculiar.

When did you ever hear of Christians wanting to dance at a funeral? There are accounts, for sure, of cannibals in America dancing a reel around the fire on which they are roasting one of their fellow-men, but I had certainly not expected to find something similar in Lutherdom. Our first death – a seaman – was interred in a Norwegian churchyard for a fee of one riksdaler. A number of his mates had smuggled a fiddle aboard the jolly-boat with them when they were accompanying him to his resting-place and scarcely had they stepped ashore than they began to trip a reel with the womenfolk. If the priest had not snatched the bow from their hands I fear that they would still have been dancing. In this behaviour it is easy to recognize what is called the East Indies *fits*.

Chapter XVII

CONCERNING A RARE FISH.

– – *dictu mirabile monstrum* – Virg.[53]

On the 25th of Feb. we sailed out on a seal hunt in the archipelago. The second assistant fired a ball at one of these sea-hounds but was unable to dive as quickly as it did and so the quarry evaded us. We landed on a small islet and, since the thaw had laid bare the odd patch of grassland, I felt the urge to become a Natural Scientist. Among the rare rocks I found here was our Swedish granite; as far as birds go, so-called common gulls were flying around by the flock; and the most remarkable plant that I encountered was the evergreen *Juniperus* or juniper bush, which the Turks keep in pots as a sacred object. Our ship's secretary, ever eager to learn, eased my toil considerably. He had found a piece of rock, egg-sized and with black stripes, which he showed me, saying it might be the strange *lapis petrificatus* or raven-stone with which it is possible to charm women to come to one at night; he had read about it in the learned author Mr *Orbis Pictor*.[54] He also found a crystallised snail that he tucked into his waistcoat pocket but he had the misfortune to be mistaken. After we had walked for a while it began to melt and trickle down his thigh, proving to be nothing but an ice-encrusted cow turd. Since he had handled it while wearing mittens, he had been unable to detect the fraud earlier. We walked on and noticed unfamiliar tracks in the snow, so my sharp-eyed companion called to our marksmen, shouting that there was an elk somewhere in the district. They came up and all of us immediately began following the tracks at a run. But to our great surprise these elk prints changed more and more into those of women's shoes. Not that the hunt was any the worse for that. We climbed out over the rocks and discovered a little cottage surrounded by some bare trees which at first had made it invisible, as if to shield its lonely tenants from the spying eyes of strangers. Our desire for natural curiosities drew us closer, and how dismayed we were when two shy nymphs, the island's sole inhabitants, fled to the woods with startled cries at the mere sight of us! We looked at one another as if to discover which of us could have such a terrifying appearance as to cause such fright. The secretary blamed it on the assistant's gun, while he in turn put the whole blame on the former's immense nose. We wanted, however, to hunt down the absconders *bongré mal-gré*[55] and our ship's pastor, who was with us, eventually inspired enough confidence with his black coat for one of them to come back, though the other sister fled the field without even looking back. She gave us some milk, as we requested, but with a hand that trembled so much that it was easy to see that she feared something. She even turned away from the proffered piece of eight with the same timidity as shown by a Swedish farmhand when offered the King's Shilling. Nor did she say anything. Our pilot told us later that they were a couple of old maids, one of whom had been unable to get a suitor while the other did not want one since she had been disappointed in her first love. Two or three times a year they come to church, otherwise they live alone in the little cabin that kinsmen had built for them. A cow and a couple of beds of herbs provide them with the necessities of life and it is unlikely that a hated male foot had ever crossed these Vestals' threshold more than this once.

Since my natural researches achieved so little success, I must bow to His Majesty of the Plant-Kingdom, Duke of Crocodiles and Mermaids, Lord of Quadrupeds, Feathered Fowl and Insects, our great knight *von Linné*, and humbly petition him to be excused these rocky excursions both here and wheresoever I may later arrive. I respect his incomparable insights and would not wish to trample to death any of his small crawling friends – nor to bend my back to look for them. For the children of mankind are my joy and, as long as I am not hated by them, I am unlikely to love the others. Besides, I feel that I was born more to enjoy nature than to admire it. I like a fragrant flower better than an unusual one, and for my admiration to fix on a beautiful rose it must be growing on the cheek of a sixteen-year-old girl.

I would, however, like to entertain von Linné just this once with an account of a little insect just as I received it from the pilots of Norway. It is the *kraken*, the so-called *crabfish*, which is said to visit these waters occasionally. It is not large since, even including the head and the tail, it is not reckoned to be any longer than our island of Öland off Kalmar.[56] All the fishermen here have something to tell about it. It keeps to the sea-bottom, perpetually surrounded by innumerable shoals of small fish that serve as its food and are then passed through it. Its mealtime, if I rightly remember what Bishop Pontoppidan wrote,[57] does not last longer than three months at a time and the following three months are spent in digesting it. During this period it feeds whole armies of smaller fish on its enormous quantities of excrement. That's why the fishermen of the country sound out its hiding place and practise their profession there to the greatest advantage. Bit by bit it rises higher and higher in the water and as soon as it has come within ten or twelve fathoms of the surface it is high time for the boats to remove themselves from the vicinity. Then, all of a sudden, it rushes up like a floating island, spurting torrents like Trollhättan from its terrible nostrils and thrashing all around so that the water whirls for miles around in great ever-widening circles. May not this creature be Job's Leviathan?[58] It would certainly be nice to have a specimen, so, if our nature-loving gentlemen would kindly book accommodation for it, we could then have it hauled hand over hand to Sweden by the remnants of our last Pomeranian Army.[59]

Chapter XVIII

PREFACE TO THE GRACIOUS READER.

Exul eram, requiesque mihi non fama petita est – Ovid.[60]

So my ink-pot has by this time already given birth to seventeen offspring, all of them lovable changelings. Now it is once again with child, probably the last of this brood.

Well, dear reader, their comic countenances have given me so much pleasure that I am now firmly resolved to declare them legitimate. At first I was minded to conceal them, as being illegitimate, far from respectable eyes but I have since hearkened to the voice of nature. My tender paternal heart will not allow me to take such a harsh course against my own children. I am thus going to declare them legitimate and entrust them to your kindly disposition.

There have been others before me who have pressed similar East Indian fosterlings into your arms but each and every one of them seems to have inherited too much of his father's earnestness. *Brelin* stands on Ascension Island and brings tears to your eyes with his lies; *Osbeck*, useful but glum, stuffs your hands full of natural curiosities; and *Torén*, more good-humoured than the others, might possibly have been able to amuse you with his pretty little acquaintances in Suratte and China but you watched as the life flowed out of him along with the last drop in his ink-pot.[61] These three are unlikely to have left behind any impressions other than tragic ones. Permit me, then, to eradicate them with my prattling progeny. I am an enemy of furrowed brows and desire only to be able to bring youth to every face.

Born of a free polity, I cannot tolerate compulsion in my studies. Scaliger[62] is as much my *bête noire* in the latter area as Machiavelli is in the former. Since the political yoke no longer burdens my shoulders, why should I have my brain burdened by a grammatical yoke? No, let the works of Donatus and Quintillianus[63] stay in the schoolroom! Rules are nothing but dead weight burdening living genius, oppressing the power of thought and limiting the quick and dashing flight of imagination. Does a ball and chain around his ankle help a runner to run?

Let genius be its own guide, then! If feelings of loftiness, beauty, nature, are not in your own soul, Aristotle is not going to impart them to you. Homer would not have been Homer if he had read our books of poetics.

Pliny the Younger speaks of an orator in his day who was very exact and regular but lacked fire and elevation: 'He has no more than one fault,' he said, 'and that is that he has nothing at all.'[64]

A face on which the hand of nature has scattered small careless attractions, as if in haste, will take possession of more hearts than the most beautiful Venus drawn with compasses and ruler.

Was Helen a beauty according to rules? If so, what fools the Greeks were to fight tooth and nail for her for all of ten years!

A speck here and there only serves to place our perfections in a clearer light. Just look at Celinde! You may be in doubt as to which adorns her more: the little black patch on her right temple or the two neighbouring shooting stars that gleam beneath the twin arches of her pretty eye-brows.

Naturam expellas furca, tamen usque recurret, as Horace says.[65] Nature floats to the top like the froth in a tankard. It is impossible for an author to hide himself on paper. His temperament stands out in everything that he writes; you could easily believe that he dips his pen in his own blood.

Where's the wonder in that? The son resembles the father, the writing the writer. How can a melancholy mind steer a light hand, or a cheerful tongue voice melancholy tones? When did you ever hear the raven call cuckoo or the cuckoo croak?

Should not each bird sing the song that suits its beak? I am more given to laughter than to weeping and would rather imitate the jollity of Scarron than the profundity of Hobbes, though elements of both are flowing in my veins.[66] Let the wine suit the bottle. I allow my mood to govern my pen and, if I am happy today and sorrowful tomorrow, you will immediately be given two chapters that reflect it.

Incarcerated for almost eighteen months on a ship and continually surrounded by wearisome monotony, may I not be permitted to seek refreshment in literary games? This sailing community measures its time according to the log-line, the trading community according to columns of figures; what would I do with my time if I were forbidden to scribble it away?

The things I am writing about are real events as I would not dare to lie when 150 eye-witnesses could stand up any day and fault me. Poetic licence may perhaps smuggle some occasionally dubious goods into my verse but my prose is utterly reliable.

I am not learned, nor do I desire the Latin placards I have hung over the threshold of each chapter to be considered as learned. But I pride myself on using them even though some modish little Mr Powder Parnassus will say that they smell of the schoolroom. I am not like a number of snobbish craftsmen who are ashamed to have their trademarks hanging over the door once they have donned a blue cloak over their apron and begun to deliberate on the Common Weal together with a table-full of political dilettantes.

We have an abundance of accounts of journeys to the East Indies, so why should I follow in the footsteps of hundreds of others? No, I shall break my own ground. I want to be new, and as proof of that I am ending this book where others would have started: I mean with the Preface to the *dear reader.*

The First Finnish Expedition

Whimsy's what I've written,
Whimsy's what I'll write.
Why should I hide from sight
The wit with which I'm smitten?

The writing suits its maker:
With the freedom of the breezes
He paints whate'er he pleases
Upon the waiting paper.

The Second Finnish Expedition
From Norway to the Cape of Good Hope

Chapter I

– *redit in tumidas naufraga puppis aquas* – Ovid.[67]

On the 6th March 1770 we congratulated each other on the favourable wind and spread our wings. By midday we were flying past Lindesnes and two days later we were swimming along between the cliffs of Shetland with joy in our hearts and a brisk wind in our sails. On the 11th we sighted Rockall, which towers like a beacon in the middle of the open sea. The Almighty seems to have expressly ordered the winds to blow for us so that we might forget our previous setbacks.

But the slow progress of our voyage earlier had sown death aboard ship. Typhus had wormed its way in below decks and in spite of the well-practised skills of our doctor we lost seven men in less than twenty days. I remember a day when we despatched three corpses over the rail at the same time. This brought distressing memories of *Finland's* misfortunes during her previous voyage, when some sort of plague had carried off pretty well half her crew in a matter of weeks, thus compelling those in command to scrape together a multi-coloured rabble in Cadiz – black, white or swarthy – to replace the dead.[68] Thanks be to God, the plague that afflicted us stopped after the seven deaths I have mentioned, though that loss was palpable enough since fate had struck at the more competent of our seamen.

To replace the boats snatched away by the hurricane of the 24th January we had negotiated the purchase of the best that was to be had in Svinörsund – that being not much more than a caulked baking-tray which, once it had been reinforced with a set of new rails, provided us with a reasonably good jolly-boat. But we still lacked a launch. So *Finland*, old woman that she was, had to produce offspring and, to the surprise of all of us, she hatched a remarkably beautiful duckling within a month. Our captain, who does not only know how to command a sailing ship but even how to build one when necessary, had a little shipyard set up in the middle of the deck. He had brought the necessary angle pieces and planks from Norway. Work started under his supervision and within a week our four carpenters had a launch on the stocks.

While they were hammering away at this new vessel, we had caught up with both summer and the trade winds. The edges of our Swedish fur-coats were already curling up and waistcoats were hardly bearable. On the 22nd we began to breathe the perpetual spring of Madeira and on the 25th we enjoyed sightings of the islands of La Palma, Gomera, Tenerife and the towering peak of the Pico. Even those in no position to see them with their eyes could smell them with their noses, so widely were the blessings of these climes distributed.

Chapter II.

FOR STRANGERS WHO WISH TO VIEW FINLAND.

-- *Vento nunc fertur amico* --[69]

A voyage in these waters is as pleasant as the weather there and may even be considered a pleasure-trip. We had the sky smiling above us, the sea gently simmering beneath us, a cooling breeze quietly murmuring and filling the belly of our sails as well as bringing health to our lungs: a climate in which the heat doesn't choke you and the cold doesn't make your teeth chatter. And all this in one place! I may add that we also had veal for our stomachs and Madeira wine for our throats. What more can a mere mortal desire?

An ambitious tyrant sailing under full sail on a sea of good fortune, an aggressor without conscience wading his way to power and riches through the tears of the oppressed, a scheming opportunist whose eyes are set on some advantageous position and who rides down more deserving applicants on the way, a debt-ridden paterfamilias who takes advantage of a favourable parliamentary wind to sail into sinecures, a young priest who, while scooting along at fifteen knots to a fat living with the help of a breeze from the court, blows away the skull-caps of a hundred grey-haired chaplains on his way – all these may think they are having a pleasurable voyage but I can assure you that my voyage in these lovely waters was even more of a joy.

I asked my friends if they had ever had a more enjoyable trip and they were unreasonable enough to answer yes. 'This is nice', they said, 'but nothing compared to the pleasure of taking a winter trip in Sweden when your sledge is pulled by a dapple-grey trotter and you overturn in a snowdrift with some little Cloris beside you.' I left them and muttered quietly to myself *Boys will have toys.*

It is easy to forget that you are at sea when everything is going so well. The ship is as steady as the earth itself and reveals any number of diverting sights without any need to look beyond the rails. Up there on the forecastle I can see a pair of sooty Cyclops hammering at an anvil so that the sparks rain down from the red-hot iron while their hammer blows are multiplied by the echo that resounds from the copper pans in the galley. If I turn towards the stern I see our worthy sailmakers bent over their work to the music of a cackling orchestra of hens, geese, capons and ducks. If I stroll to the mainmast I can see a small boat growing at the hands of our industrious carpenters, and a little further on ropes and yarns are being spun along with the tail-ends of stories, frayed lies, threads of gossip and even, now and again, reels and dances.(h) If I lean over the rail my eye perceives a shoal of hungry sharks at the surface of the water and, in among them, dolphins and porpoises. If I look up at the foretop I have to laugh at the look-out who is shouting that he can see a sailing ship port of the sun or starboard of his nose.(i)

But there is so much more here worthy of note. Would you like to accompany me below deck, Sir? – Good. – The Finnish gentry live back here at the stern, don't you know? This is the cabin where the Literary Society meets twice a week.(k) Next door is where we drink when there is a name-day. Over there lives the fellow who murders folk and right alongside him the one who buries them. This chest (l) with the sailcloth over it contains death and life, since it serves as both as medicine chest and pulpit. – But shall we continue? Let's go along Port Street first. – Watch out for the hammocks; they're alive, and you can easily end up in a scrap with one of the coastguards lurking in them. – This is the second table, and it is here that Mr D. was fined five pieces of eight after being unable to consume three hens in one meal as he had wagered. – There is a smaller table behind it, which is where the midshipmen eat peas and squabble. – Along here on the right you can see 50 sheep, which from time to time are abruptly removed from this toilsome world and given an honourable burial in our stomachs. Right opposite is where their dear relatives the goats live, as well as all kinds of swine. And here you can see the ship's splendid wet-nurse, a worthy bovine matron from Hisingen and sister of the heavy ox that the district judge received from that prudent Dane J.P. as an inducement to promote him to Member of Parliament in 1765. Her last son has already gone to eternity via the hands of the cook. She gives us milk daily, which is why we spare her flesh. – These small round things are called plums aboard ship – you'll notice a number of them in D.'s collection of natural curiosities. – Come a little farther forward now, even though it's smoky. This is the kitchen – that stove at the front is for the officers' table and that enormous copper pan behind it is for cooking the rations for all the messmates.- Stop, stop! Don't go in there, Sir! That's the privy! – Now, let's go back along Starboard Street. Under there you can see three oxen. Contemplate them – and the patience with which they bear their horns! If you want to see our sheet anchor, that's it. If you were to make it fast to the moon, I'm certain we could haul it down from the sky. – Can you hear that noise from below the deck, as if the chests themselves were alive? That's two seamen who have drunk each other's schnapps and are now quarrelling about it. – That fellow laughing at them with dribble coming out of his mouth is our carpenter, and the other one with the tankard in his paw is a Finn who dances a bear dance as soon as you give him a dram. As you pass along here, put your hands over your ears for there is a chap learning to play the fiddle. – Forgive me, my dear fellow, I can't accompany you any further: I need to get some fresher air into my lungs, and my thirst is reminding me that I need to look up today's name-day in my almanac in order to find a reason for quenching it.

h) Up on the forecastle, which might be called the Finnish Gossip Square.
i) Port and starboard are equivalent to left and right.
k) See Chapters 7, 8, 9.
l) The medicine chest, from which the sermons were preached on the outward journey.

Chapter III

WHICH BEGINS WITH 11,000 VIRGINS AND ENDS WITH A FIGHT.

Fecundi calices, quem non fecere disertum? Horace.[70]

Hello there, Brother Bibbers, Chevaliers of the Arrack Bottle and the Ale Stoup! Which name-day are we celebrating today? What does the almanac say? Eleven Thousand Virgins' Day – - ha, ha! There are scarcely that many virginal creatures in the whole of popery. It must be a monkish lie. Nevertheless, we are told that they all became martyrs on this one day, so let's have a wake! The first toast is to them:

> Well, Brother Bacchants, ancient legends tell us
> Eleven thousand virgins perished on this day,
> Put to the sword if we believe those monkish fellows,
> Put to the soldiery seems to me the likelier way.
> For when virgins fall they rise in different guise,
> 'Tis a wound that's rarely fatal, with little loss of blood.
> So, Brothers of our Order, fill your glasses and arise,
> Let us wash their lovely bodies in a tearful grapy flood!
> Weep, punchbowl, weep tears that fill our glasses
> And help the flow of our funerary feast.
> 'Tis the poorest mourner who drinks the least,
> So cheers to all the martyred lasses
> Who passed away as virgins and rose as something else!

What's it to be next? The welfare of *Finland*!

> *Finland*, thou matron that we hold dear,
> We toast thee that all may hear.
> To thy success each man will pour
> Wine down his gullet till it holds no more.
> May following winds e'er bless thy way
> Across the realm where fish hold sway!
> May currents, oceans, stormy blasts
> Ne'er threaten more thy trusty masts!
> May hunger, thirst and sickness vile
> Ne'er plague thy floating Finnish isle!
> And, dear mother, just one thing more:
> Do not take us to Pul-candor! (m)

What now, gentlemen? Aren't you going to drink a toast?(n) Fie! It's a vulgar habit invented originally by lewd Circe, who thereby transformed Ulysses' companions into pigs.[71] It was then taken up anew by London coal-heavers during the Wilkesian disturbances and is now only practised at foul nocturnal meetings in Wapping and Westminster.[72]

It has, however, been adopted by most of Gothenburg, including the fair sex.

Not true, not true, gentlemen! Don't denigrate our womenfolk to that extent! I presume you are only referring to the inmates of the workhouse. How could I possibly imagine that a respectable girl would transform the bloom of her pretty cheeks to chapped red pockmarks by drinking filthy toasts, or turn her sweet pink lips into dribbling wine-pipes?

Who said they were to drink that much? But two or three glasses won't hurt, especially as Gothenburg women tend to be on the pale side and a drop of wine might defy nature and produce roses where they might otherwise not flower.

And what roses! They are what I call booze blemishes. But if you want to turn their faces purple, you only have to come out with toasts consisting of such Scottish pleasantries as: *pr-- and purse never failing — black c-- and white tighs* etc. There's not a girl alive who wouldn't blush at such coarseness.

What do you mean blush? – I have seen them smile at such things. – And I could name both married women and misses who've made me toasts such as – –

No examples, you rogue! Truth should be told on all possible occasions but, when it's a matter of the honour of womenfolk, the slightest breath of the truth merits a thrashing. – A thrashing? – Quite, a thrashing. – Huh, watch what you're saying! Or you'll – – Stop! Watch the punchbowl – Damn and blast you. – Now look at the glassware – Ha, ha, ha, what a to-do!

Who is right, dear reader? Shouldn't these drinking duels be punished as severely as those with the sword? I don't know which is the more pitiful sight: a defeated duellist rolling around in his blood or a drunk in his vomit. I have seen a toasting hero drink twenty or thirty glasses without a break between them, and this is supposed to be in honour of a girl! Who is crazier: someone like that or Don Quixote, who fasted for four days and nights beneath the open sky for his Dulcinea del Toboso? Oh, if I were Celinda and my Damon assaulted his health in that way in my name, I can assure you that he would not enjoy a single favourable glance until all twenty glasses had poured from his eyes as tears of honest remorse. I shall for my part not desist from deprecating this custom as long as it has defenders. And I certainly shan't leave it unchallenged on this ship.

m) In the China Sea, where the ship was forced to linger on its last voyage.
n) *Toast*, a sort of drinking duel introduced by the English, in which two or more men compete to discover which of them should have the honour of being drunker for the sake of a particular girl.

Chapter IV

THE BEGINNING OF A SPLENDID COLLECTION OF NATURAL CURIOSITIES.

Ridetur, chorda, qui semper oberrat eadem – Horace.[73]

There was an abundance of all kinds of swimming and flying species to be seen here but why should I describe anything that is not fit for eating? In my opinion the farmer's barn is the most beautiful menagerie of all, for which is of more value – the ox or the crocodile, the sheep or the tiger? I had tears in my eyes when I saw an all-devouring host of lions, bears and ostriches being supported at the king's expense in the menagerie at Versailles while hundreds of starving Frenchmen ran around begging on the streets of Paris. And I was angry with myself in London for admiring an array of stuffed rarities in the British Museum more than the nutritious armies of oxen that were daily driven past my windows on their way to the slaughterhouse. When I considered how the latter satisfied a million hungry stomachs whereas the former only provided pleasure for the eyes of the curious few, it seemed to me that I was guilty of the sin of ingratitude towards Nature herself by paying more attention to what was rare than to what was useful.

Learned men travel to the East Indies to collect natural curiosities; crafty chaps go there to earn money; but I, being neither the one nor the other, am quite simply travelling to make a living. If I wanted a collection of curiosities I would choose that of the farmer. A barn full of cows, sheep, horses, pigs, hens etc. is something I consider worth the trouble of acquiring.

Nevertheless (notice how quickly I change horses - you could take me for a politician), nevertheless, I am thinking of putting together a small cabinet of animals, though quite unlike those of my worthy predecessors in that I intend to describe the souls of my small animals whereas others have restricted themselves to the bodies. I shall investigate their moral characteristics whereas others have not gone beyond the natural sphere. In short, I want to get to the heart of the matter. Let others stick to the fins and tails as long as they want to. I shall thus be opening up a new field of learning and I hope to attract more attention to myself as a result.

This is what the *flying fish* looks like - a brother to Sister Bat ashore. Both are ill-conceived on the part of nature. Jove, so the sea chronicle says, sat down to create them and intended that both of them should be birds but his jealous consort Juno pinched his ear just at that moment. 'Ouch! Leave off!' shouted the old man in surprise and let the half-finished work slip from his hands. One fell into the sea and the other landed on land.

The moral character of the flying fish is frenetic and given to excess, for it plays all kinds of tricks on the surface of the water and sometimes even ventures right up into the air. It is on such occasions that we get them on deck, where they fall and die as soon as their wing-fins dry out.

I intend to take a specimen of this fish home with me, above all to demonstrate how worthless the promises of poets are when they swear to some vain Maecenas from whom they have managed to wheedle benefit:[74]

Fish will learn to fly
before I forget your favour etc.

Also, to remind a number of my powdered fellow-citizens in Sweden – especially young men in commerce – not to fly higher than their wings can carry them. 'Look', I shall say pointing to my fish, 'this little creature would still have been alive if it had kept closer to the ground.'

Here you can see a *booby*, probably the most stupid of all birds, slightly larger than a kite and full of black vermin. The sailors can catch it with their bare hands. One evening one of the seamen took one of them on the big lantern we have at the stern.

I immediately examined its moral characteristics and found it to be very like one of those be-aproned Master Craftsmen ashore who run from their last or needle to political drinking sessions. For it is foolhardy, it is worthless, it is lousy, it screams a great deal and it leaves its dirt behind it on the spars and yards it has been sitting on, just like a boozy armchair politician when, pipe in one hand and *Post and Gazette* in the other, he rests his patched elbow on the table in the dregs of cheap booze and tobacco ash.

This bird would be very suitable as a sign hanging over the door of one of those little ale-clubs for political dabblers that we have at home. It would at least be more natural than seeing two stern, gilded lions holding a pair of tailor's shears between them and standing above the inscription *Die Schneider-gesellen ihre Herberge.*[75]

This bird, however, is called *malefit*[76] or malefactor, a nickname it has been given by superstitious sailors, who accuse it of being a portent of storms. But the bird is wholly innocent in that respect and I have observed that it just as often brings sunshine as bad weather.

I shall include it in my collection not in order to describe its vices or its virtues – for it has neither – but to draw attention to prejudice and superstition. When the cock crows in the evening there is always some aged crone who prophesies a misfortune in the district, and dear old Grandma would never dream of losing a tooth without imagining that someone in the family is going to die. 'Pay attention now, old wifies', I shall say to them when they look at my bird, 'your cocks crow when they can't sleep and your rotten teeth fall out when you've done too much gossiping. But they don't portend either misfortune or death.' My *malefit* brought a favourable wind with it even though the sailors imagined with dread that it would bring a storm.

This is a Portuguese man-of-war, a strange beast. The sea chronicle I mentioned earlier informs us that it was created as an ordinary fish in the first place but afterwards demanded a different and more fashionable form since it was annoyed at resembling the common fishy mob. Jove was so enraged by this that he hurled it back into the sea in the shape it now reveals to us. Governed by its earlier taste for contradiction, the man-of-war permanently sails against both winds and current. It resembles nothing but itself, and it seems to be nothing more than slime inflated by the wind.

Nature, who seems sometimes to be playing with her creations, has probably developed this animal in order to have some creature on the water that resembles our so-called *freethinkers* ashore, for the latter too, with their manic itch to be new and unusual, are perpetually swimming against the current. The Bible is too old and therefore it is no longer of any use. They do not understand the soul so it is the body that does the thinking. Hell is a thousand year old fable to terrify the superstitious common people. And why should they go to church when everyone else does? They want to have a God but they can't bear having the one who is worshipped by the common herd. What a splendid philosophy!

If any of them were to honour my collection of natural curiosities with an interested glance, I would shrug my shoulders, weep and sigh: Oh, you Portuguese man-of-war!

Chapter V

AN APPENDIX TO THE FOREGOING. CONCERNING THE WOLF OF THE SEA.

- Escarum horrenda vorago -
Poscit quod pontus, quod terra, quod educat aer – Ovid.[77]

What a stupendous carcass! A shark heavier than the mightiest Småland ox. Only with difficulty can thirty men hoist him on deck. The whole of my cabin is no larger than his awe-inspiring gullet. This, without doubt, was the prophet's whale.

Such were the thoughts that stormed through my head when I saw this thug of the sea for the first time. The bear in the forest is less unpleasant than the shark in the sea. The one we had just caught measured twelve feet in length and his circumference was almost the same. He looked as if he could swallow a dragoon whole since his jaws accounted for a third of his body. Four carpenters set to with axes and opened great holes in him both to port and to starboard and blood flowed around the deck from them in long vile streams. We have caught several smaller ones since but never one to equal this one. The following drawing shows him at full stretch.

A smallish shark from the side.

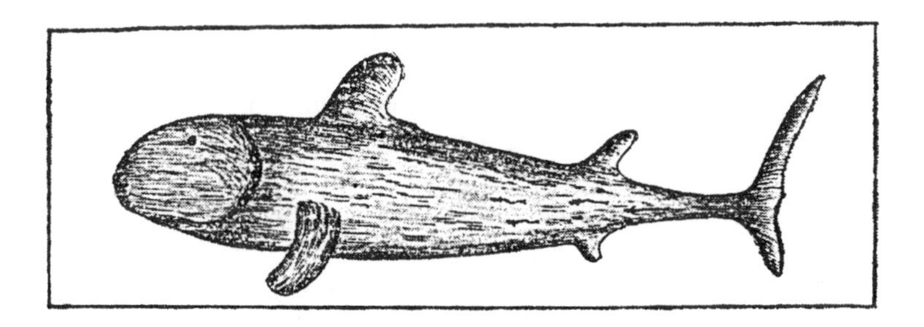

The shark is the most voracious predator in the ocean realm. He hangs back in the wash like a lurking salvage man and accepts everything that is thrown overboard: hens that fall asleep, suicidal pigs, old cow-dung, ox-tripe, shoulders of mutton, baggy trousers and the rest – which is why the Dutch call him *Struntfreter*.[78] He has a particularly enjoyable meal when a human being slips over the rail. Our sailors say that the arrival of the shark means that someone on the ship is going to die and they claim that he is out there waiting for Christian flesh. They are, consequently, his bitterest enemies and will happily put their own ration of pork on the hook in order to catch him. If they succeed – and they rarely fail since he is such a glutton that he chases the bait even when the hook has already drawn blood from him several times – they cut off his tail and fins and, having thus mutilated the poor brute, they toss him back into the sea where he threshes about like a storm-damaged Algerian galley without rudder and oars. Sometimes they lash an old ship's barrel on him and laugh heartily at his fruitless attempts to dive. English sailors take their vengeance even further: they treat sharks according to *jus talionis*[79] and eat them when they catch them.

I have seen this fish still alive even after being flayed. The skin, when dried, is used for rasps and files. The jaws, which are actually situated under the head, have three rows of sharp teeth and anyone who accidentally sticks his foot in can be sure of going through life on a wooden leg: no razor has a better edge. The shark does not produce roe as ordinary fish do – instead it produces young in the same way as mammals. Our doctor preserved its brain. He also showed me something so strange that I do not think it exists elsewhere in the whole of nature: there were two *penes* on the one body.

We can gather something about the moral character of the shark from all this. His predatory sorties aft of the ship demonstrate a merciless lust for shipwrecks. If I could get my hands on the salvage inspectors over on the coast of Jutland, I would slap them in the face with a shark's tail and say: 'You Jutlanders, you are truly nothing but godless sharks!' For when they pray to the Lord to bless their shores, they do not mean with cod, herring and ling but with large, richly-laden vessels that they can sack under the euphemistic name of Christian salvage. The diving-bell is by far their most productive fishing net. On my return journey from London in 1769, I saw two vessels stranded on Skagen [80] – a Russian man o'war and a little cargo boat. The prospects for the latter were painful to contemplate. When I looked at the former, however, I recalled the words of Diogenes [81] when he observed the woman who had hanged herself in the forest: 'Oh that all trees might bear such fruit'. They are welcome to take the reckless troublemakers but never let a peaceful merchantman fall into their clutches!

More about the character of the shark. His repeated attacks on the waiting hook reveal an untamed desire for sensual pleasure. He does not draw back from the danger even when there is blood gushing from his throat. The iron has already gouged a deep furrow in his gum and yet he returns only to become at last an unhappy victim of his own gluttony. How like our idle human voluptuaries in that respect! Do you know the lard-stuffed *Herr von Guzzle* and his uncle *Aleberg* with the huge copper-coloured nose? The stomach of the one has ached a hundred times from the burden of unnecessary meals, and the other's head has just as often sagged from the nightly torments of intoxication. But do you imagine they guzzle and swill any the less for that? No! For they have the character of the shark. What happened to poor Corydon, that lovable youth who was supposed to be a joy to his parents? He wanted to travel. His mother's farewell kiss was accompanied by tears and his father said: 'My son, keep God before your eyes.' Corydon arrived in Cadiz, and left there with the burning sores of careless lust. He was cured, but arrived in China and sinned anew. What more is to be said? Corydon died – Corydon, that lovable youth who was to be a joy to his parents, met his death in the bosom of a heathen, like a pretty flower that, pierced at its root by a poisonous asp, fades away and disappears in its most hopeful morning hour.

Poor wretches! Pitiable brothers of the shark! Why do you pick roses from a bush that has recently torn your hands? Voluptuousness undermines life just as a mole undermines trees. Consider the fate of the shark and tremble!

As a final observation on this brutal fish I should mention that he has even learned the art of living on the death of others. Everything in the above description supports this: a corpse has no sooner gone over the rail than the shark is feasting on it with delight.

Greedy heirs who, smiling at the gravesides of their fathers, divide the inheritance for which they have waited so long; the lowly official who waits the very life out of his superior and ascends triumphant upon his coffin; the twenty-year-old widow who, having enticed a good will out of her dying old husband, shares it with an old flame: tell me, dear reader, whether these are one jot better than my wolf of the sea?

Chapter VI

A REMARKABLE MEETING BETWEEN THE SHIP FINLAND AND A PIRATE.

Arma virumque cano – - Virg.[82]

While I was collecting natural curiosities in this way we reached the vicinity of the line. I cannot describe every single sailing vessel that came into sight on our way since it is only with curiosities that my quill is concerned. I shall therefore immediately betake myself to the scene of a battle so that my ink may mix with the blood of the combatants.

On Good Friday 1770 the rising sun revealed to us an unknown ship that was cruising back and forth and gradually approaching us closer and closer. Since we were peacefully preparing to start our church service nothing could have been further from our minds than war, but this strange tacking, first to one side of us then to the other, made us justifiably suspicious. We raised the Swedish flag, hoping thereby to bring out his flag, but in vain. I immediately took him for a pirate since the cook had dreamed the night before that someone hit him in the face with potatoes and the carpenter swore that the blood-red auroras we had seen farther north could not mean anything other than war.

So as not to be surprised by an ambush, *Finland* was made ready to defend herself. The hymn book was put away and the ramrod taken out in its place. In no time at all we had 140 warriors standing there armed and death was all ready to roar from the sixteen gunports on each side. Bandages and plasters lay ready for the wounded, and I must state in honour of my countrymen that they all waited for the order to attack with expressions worthy of the warriors of King Karl XII.

I for my part had long been desirous of warlike adventures and was thus joyfully prepared to accept this opportunity to satisfy my longing. Certain in the knowledge that a bullet is most likely to strike the man who is fearful, I decided not to remain in the powder magazine. Never having read recent Swedish history I consequently did not understand how anyone could receive the wounds of battle in his back, especially as I had observed that my grandfather – an old, grey-haired follower of King Karl – carried all his on his front. Were I to live for a hundred years I should never forget what the old man reminded me the last time I visited him in this world. I was a boy of ten: 'Listen, boy', he said and grasped my shoulder with a hand that seemed to swallow up half of my small person, 'listen, if you ever get into danger, stare it straight in the face for it respects a bold appearance. You will be lost if you turn your face away. King Karl, God bless his soul' – here the old man dried his eyes – 'when he led us into battle to teach the Russians a lesson' – here he stroked his moustaches and looked stern – 'and we slaughtered them like oxen' – here he gave another hearty smile – 'and waded up to the knees of our boots in blood – it was a very small number that fell in the battle itself. Let me tell you, my boy, that the greatest losses are always among those who take to their heels. The more you run away, the closer death dogs your footsteps. So stand like a man!'

I now recalled what he had told me and determined to act

accordingly. Poor old fellow! He was in good health right up to 1742 when he read in the *Post* that the Russians had won their victory at Helsinki by using Swedish cannon. At this he took a stroke and died.

As soon as I saw the preparations for war begin in earnest I recalled how the generals of old had spurred on their warriors with an exhortatory address. In order to have one ready in case of need I went below and composed the following lines in great haste:

> Rise, Finland's children bold, and shrug off your petty fear!
> Remember honour, freedom, life itself! A pirate ship draws near!
> Up, arm yourselves, prepare, cloak every limb in iron mail,
> 'Tis farewell to our money chests should our defences fail.
> Should shameless rascals dare approach us on the deep,
> Consume our victuals, drink our schnapps, fleece us as we fleece
> sheep?
> Should we, as slaves, be carried to some isle across the foam,
> Torn from the bosoms we hold dear, of girls, of friends, of home?
> No! I'll smile at every fatal shot, in death itself delight
> As long as pirate's gore with mine is mingled in my sight.
> My spirit, freed, will leave my corpse, forgetting every sore
> If I can bear along with me one buccaneer or more.
> Remember now your Swedish birth, give proof to all this day
> That heroes' blood, inherited, is flowing in your veins.
> Stand face to face, not back to back, as may be done by some:
> A hero's wounded in the front, a coward in the bum.
> He comes for prey, this pirate shark, but we shall make him taste
> The rapier blade of justice grim long e'er he flees in haste.
> Take down the thund'ring muskets, keep steady hand and nerve
> To blast this pack of vermin to the hell they all deserve.
> Let cannon crash and musket flash and sword blade ring aloud,
> The noise alone will cause them quake and make the deep resound.
> 'Tis the bold who carry off the prize, naught is the coward's lot,
> And victory's wreathe oft crowns the brow that fires the first shot.

My heart leapt at the great deeds we were to perform. There can be no doubt, I thought, that this rascal will have in tow an abducted beauty who is pining for her freedom. Who knows, it might be an

African princess who was bathing with her playful maidens in a calm river one still and lonely eve, or sitting under a shady palm on the shore of a gently murmuring lake, sorrowing for the absence of her beloved and all the while mingling her sighs with the mournful tones of the turtle-dove or seeking sympathy from the imitative echoes from the forest. I mentioned my guesses to my friends and we all hoped to acquire a Banise.[83] What an honour, we said one to the other, to rescue suffering innocence and to hear a princess call us her protectors while her nymphs kneel before us and greet us as heroes. Meanwhile, we shall be stuffing one pirate after the other into our cannon and blasting them all the way to the kingdom of the dead!

The outline of an heroic epic was already forming in my imagination. At least, I thought, this example of Swedish heroism will not be buried in oblivion. Voltaire writes in his *Henriade*:[84]

Les Francois savent vaincre et chanter leurs victoires.

I have found that, however much we may surpass all other nations in the former, we fail in the latter and thus there is no country that can boast of more Achilles and fewer Iliads than ours.

Filled as I was with such notions I was delighted to hear the order to attack. As is customary according to the laws of war we questioned the privateer whether he wanted to surrender or fight by sending a cannonball across his bows. We were now so close that by using small telescopes we could see the faces of the enemy on deck and among them we even discovered six or seven skirts. There we had the handmaidens of our African princess! What a spur to the courage of our young men! The crack of our greeting drove them headlong down into the bowels of the ship but the mere sight of them had the effect of causing us to shout as one man 'Fire!' But just at that moment the whole blessed vessel turned broadside on and the enemy (damn him – he might have shown some desire to fight!) raised the English flag, lowered sail and hove to, sending us over a couple of hundred potatoes (as the cook had dreamt) instead of the chainshot we expected.

Alas, dear reader, judge my disappointment from your own! All of my novel, princess, nymphs, victory, booty, heroic epic – the whole lot lost in the twinkling of an eye. Peace wafted all round us. Like a miser who has found a bag of ducats in his sleep and wakes to find an empty nightcap in his hand, I crept down to my cabin with my nose quite out of joint. My pen was thus the only thing to bleed in this war.

Our pirate was a Captain Laner from London and the moon must have been his destination since the place he mentioned is not to be found on the globe. It was impossible to know his true intentions but we guessed that he was cruising these latitudes in order to meet English East Indiamen. We therefore invited him aboard for dinner in the hope of being able to send mail to Europe with him. He came, accepted our letters and received a quarter barrel of herring in exchange for his potatoes. The women he had aboard were a number of ladies of easy virtue from Westminster who presumably preferred to populate the colonies than to spin in Brideswell.[85] See my chapter on ship's rats. Black or white, the Englishman has to have something.

Chapter VII

WHICH WILL SERVE AS A PORCH TO WHAT FOLLOWS.

Inter Sauromatas ingeniosus eram -- Ovid.[86]

We roasted for eleven days below the line in a languorous heat. In the old days the dog star went to the heads of East Indiamen in these regions and they used to duck each other, play the fool and get drunk, but on this occasion they were under orders to keep their wits about them and so they are all still of sound mind.

To make up for the loss of the fun and games I had started to publish a weekly journal with the title of *The Swedenborgian Post.* It consisted of all kinds of political and historical reports from Europe reported to me by various willing spirits who sometimes manifested themselves in the cabin on *Finland* formerly occupied by Secretary E. But it seems that everything that appears with such a title is doomed to inevitable failure. Neither the judges in Sweden nor their familiars aboard ship truly respect the law regarding press freedom. The paper had to close after its first two editions.

The same thing happened here, however, as when you play Campio: the knave always brings another card along with him. My example set the pens to work. The ink sluices opened and floods of literary efforts swamped the benches and tables. Someone produced a *Neptune's Spy*, someone else entertained us with *The Finnish Post*. Some corresponded in rhyme, others began to write novels. There wasn't a name-day or a birthday that was allowed to pass without greetings. The poetic vein flowed all the more freely from being lubricated with the juices of arrack. In short, every brain was pregnant to popping point. No sooner was the plug pulled out of the inkwell than out crept a *bel esprit*.

But children soon tire of the same toy. The whole storehouse of our learning tumbled down within three weeks, though a new Phoenix grew from its rubble in that the assemblage of gentleman authors decided to form a Literary Society with the name *Runio Sacrum*, that particular Swedish poet seeming to be the most suitable patron.[87] A design for the society's shield was sketched by our worthy member Mr Ad. Burtz; it depicts the aforementioned *Runius* drunk and lying in a gutter while three ladies, visible in a window, are asking him to compose. Above them is inscribed the following motto:

Oh, what a pretty pattern!
One window with three slatterns.

I had the honour to be elected secretary of the society. The meetings were to be held twice a week and each member in turn was to be chairman and open the sitting with a toast to the memory of Runius, after which the toasts would proceed round the whole table. I dare not reveal the arcane mysteries of the society but I shall give a short account of the rest of its history in the chapters that follow.

Chapter VIII

CONCERNING THE LITERARY SOCIETY RUNIO SACRUM.

Adsit laetitiae Bacchus dator --[88]

At our first meeting the preliminary question raised was whether there was necessarily a connection between the nerves of the brain and the fibres in the throat. The matter was examined and it was concluded that dehydration of the latter prevents the expansion of the former, thus rendering them incapable of functioning properly. This was explained by analogy with a mill, which is incapable of grinding corn without water, and by the case of Runius and a number of others. It was decided that genius unequivocally requires the support of the punchbowl.

The second question arose naturally from the first: did the assembled gentlemen possess a supply of lemons, sugar and arrack? The majority answered in the affirmative. The rest were declared ineligible for membership of our society and departed.

This accomplished, the next question was whether all were prepared to write about, or allow to be written about, any topic which might in the future be proposed. There was unanimous consent, whereafter the society sat down to discuss and settle its laws, of which I shall only mention the principal ones.

III. The table being fully occupied, the chairman shall announce a topic for the next sitting and it is on this that all must write. There shall be freedom in the choice of fixed or free form. Should anyone raise an objection, the objector is to be fined one ladle of punch.

V. No one shall fail to attend when he has been summoned by the messenger. The fine to be two bottles on the first occasion, double that on the second. If he be ill, the fine for that illness to be a loaf of sugar.

VII. The chairman shall decide who wins the prize. The best contribution to be rewarded with eight glasses and the second best with four glasses.

X. In the case of slander by one member upon another: if that slander be perpetrated in prose the fine shall be as for absence under paragraph V; if that slander be in verse there shall be no case to answer.

Last. In consideration of the necessity of replenishing the vessel containing all fines levied, it is the duty of each and every member to ensure that at suitable intervals he be in breach of the prescribed paragraphs. Signed in our meeting place aboard *Finland* this the 1st day of April in the year of Our Lord 1770.

Johan Innshield — Adam Flaskfield
Peter Coldram — Jöns Dribblestream
L.S.
Truls Inkwell
(Secretary)

A society organized so judiciously could not fail to produce things of beauty and I would have expatiated in praise of all the gentlemen involved were it not that paeans to the living might be thought of as flattery. It is my duty, however, to offer one or two samples of our literary output, especially such as were awarded prizes.

The first topic set was *Love in infant guise*, on which a goodly amount was written. I offer only the shortest of the pieces here.

The First Motto.
---- *pedibus calcamus amorem* -[89]

What is *love in infant guise*?
A scorpion's egg to blight the morrow,
A snare to trap the not yet wise,
A madhouse mark of future sorrow.

To H-- with torment for a girl!
Should Amor greet me when I land,
Bacchus' spigot I shall hurl
And sweep the bow far from his hand.

The Second Motto.

Each bird sings according to its beak.

I can hardly claim to treat
Of what love is in infant guise.
As I recall from times gone by
I merely felt an awful heat
Whene'er dear Greta I did meet:
No more than that did ardour rise.
  So I guess the guise of love
  Was all innocent like a dove.
Since those days my eager hands
Have learnt to seek out hidden lands,
My lips are now inclined to tarry,
My heart to beat all in a flurry
With violent changes, fast and slow,
That make me shake from head to toe.
  So I guess the guise of love
  Is manly now, unlike the dove.

Do not be indignant, dear reader. These efforts are no more to my taste than they are to yours but it is my duty as an historian to include them. In order to give you some satisfaction I shall now show you a different piece that, in a quite masterly fashion, struggles with the ambiguity of the set topic. His motto was:

What Was My Son Doing on the Galley?

Cadiz was the scene of the tale,
'Twould make his dear mother's heart quail,
Where young Crispin rolled with some tarts.
'Twas a wonderful night that he had
– So he said – until the poor lad
Felt the start of a smart in his parts.

Listen Doctor, he whispered so low,
I've a small sore somewhere below,
Can you help e'er it doubles in size?
I asked the old quack if he knew
What made Crispin so pallid a hue.
Being wise, he surmised it was love in disguise.

The assembled company, even though it had expected the subject to be treated differently, considered itself more than indebted to the author for his tasteful treatment of a tasteless matter and awarded him the prize, which consisted of eight glasses of Bishop's Punch that the chairman passed to him after a speech suitable to the occasion. The poet accepted them with a bow and the following ditty:

If a wheel
Tends to squeal
You should often oil it.
If you don't,
Can't or won't,
You will surely spoil it.

Likewise ought
A thirsty throat
Be offered lubrication.
I am sure
Spirit pure
Oils the inspiration.

Someone else had taken the opportunity to scrape together various indecent pieces in the style of Rochester [90] in an attempt to prove that love is no more than a violent hunger for a piece of beautiful white *womanflesh*. The effort was witty enough in its way but the society did not feel justified in preserving a couple of hundredweight of crudity among its papers for the sake of its two or three grains of genius. The author was consequently sentenced to make his peace with respectability by supplying two bowls of punch at the next meeting.

Chapter IX

FURTHER REMARKS ON RUNIO SACRUM.

Sive recta sive crum,
Tamen est latinicum. [91]

I have read through the foregoing chapter and I do not like it since it seems excessively lewd. I had therefore considered doing away with it had it not occurred to me in the interim that drinking is as necessary an evil at sea as marriage is ashore. The one produces courage in the midst of dangers, the other comfort in the midst of labours. Neither of them can be dispensed with. What is it that makes such daring seamen of the English? Nothing but their great goblets of wine and mugs of ale. If you see one of their captains with a lean and pale visage you may be sure that he is not performing any seafaring miracles; but if he has a nose so huge, red and chapped that you think it would make a veritable inn sign, you may assume that he is a true hero of the realm of Neptune. Just as we Swedes have not yet achieved their prominence in the art of drinking, so do we lag equally far behind them when it comes to worldwide voyages. No one will be surprised, then, that East Indiamen seek strength in the punchbowl.

It is, however, a matter of being able to drink with refinement. In the old days people got drunk in the blunt old peasant fashion. Now you will find that it happens in a cultured and civilized way. That's a great change for the better. An evil that cannot be abolished should at least be made as tolerable as possible. It is this noble precept that drives our worthy society *Runio sacrum.*

Why then should I be ashamed to write its history? But, dear reader, I happen to have two stronger reasons for not completing it:

firstly, I have nothing to drink, and secondly, I can't be bothered. So you are not going to get more than one more page at most, and it is likely to be so pathetic that you will consider your loss a fortunate one.

The following effort won the prize at our third session. The question was: What will your future wife look like?

Motto:
Chacun a son goût.[92]

If I should ever fall in love
Here is the girl that I would have:
Of middling height, she'll walk with free and lively gait;
Artlessly pretty, with control but no constraint.
Of complexion firm and clear shot with the glow of health,
Pink flecks on a snowy landscape like spring flowers growing in stealth.

A pair of rosy lips that can form a pretty smile
Or sing a song or kiss in a way that still lacks guile.
Her eyes are merry, full of fire, but withal innocent
Beneath their arches that like two Cupid's bows are bent.
Her breasts are high and though, like marble, firm and white
Still ever kindle fire to keep us warm at night.
With such a body and, of course, a soul
She can make of me her thrall.
That's the sort of girl for this man
And once I've found her I plan
To sacrifice my freedom.

Poor lad! Are you ever likely to get married? – At our fifth meeting everyone was invited to proclaim what he was primarily interested in. Money had many adherents, honour one, learning none. Two announced that they were for a little of everything but the prize went this time to the one who composed in praise of sensual pleasure. He called himself:

Epicuri de grege porcus [93]

Come, Voluptua, goddess mine,
Come, overpower my eager soul!
For you alone my heart does pine,
To you I raise the sacrificial bowl.
Buried 'twixt your breasts so white
I laugh at Croesus' gold and Alexander's might.
Ambitious fools may climb the cliffs of fortune
But sorrow, envy, toil alone will be their portion.
Let glutton fill his plate, and fill it thrice again,
He merely feeds the serpent that is gnawing at his brain.
But you, Voluptua, you alone can veil
The thistle path with fragrance sweet
And sensual pleasure: balm to feet
That tread barefoot through life's dark vale.
Fields Elysian may well await us
But the best will then be missing:
There will be no wine to sate us,
And I doubt there'll be much kissing.

Verse of this kind, stated our secretary, could never be the offspring of a sober mind and it was his submission that the chair should examine with care the extent to which this author's delirious genius should be encouraged by the award of further quantities of the same intoxicating substance; he, for his part, considered that it could only be damaging. He therefore recommended that the prize due to the poet should be converted from punch to an equivalent quantity of water, that being of most service to his befuddled head. – This concern for a sick brother was interpreted as a gross calumny. The secretary was driven from his minutes and compelled to defend himself behind a rampart of three bottles of red wine, which he handed over for distribution.

In this manner the society continued with it meetings until we were approaching the Cape, at which point its literary activities as well as the remnants of arrack and sugar came to an end. I rounded off its proceedings with the following swan-song:

> O, coup fatal pour les buveurs
> De notre heureuse compagnie!
> Adieu bouteille, adieu ma vie!
> Voici ton secreteur en pleurs,
> Bacchus, tous tes sujets fidels,
> dont le courage et la constance
> furent l'appui de ta puissance,
> ne brulent plus sur tes autels.[94]

I could, of course, append the reports of a couple of extraordinary baronial courts that were in session during the same period in order to try sundry of cases of intercourse with the daughters of Norway etc., but I haven't got the energy. Apart from which I'm not sure that I shouldn't draw a veil of respectability over such very natural cases.

Claudite jam rivos, pueri, sat prata bibere. Virg.[95]

Chapter X

THE CONTENTS OF WHICH I SHALL STATE WHEN IT IS WRITTEN.

Qualis rex, talis grex -[96]

I recall that someone in Stockholm converted *Literary Society* into *Sily Irate Cotery* by means of an anagram. I mention this merely to save any splitter of hairs the trouble of applying the same approach to our society. What we wrote may have been indifferent but at least it was short; a courtesy that the reader won't receive from all hawkers of literary wares.

Our captain, however, had made better use of his leisure hours in the trade-wind zone by translating a nice English book called

Henrietta.[97] Not that he merits nomination as an honoured member of the Swedish Academy of Sciences except by comparison with our scribblings, but it does serve as proof that genius, which is usually hidden away by the sons of Neptune as something shameful, was held in some respect on this voyage. That we drank was our own doing; that we were practitioners of the pen was a consequence of his example. How dreadful it would be to be tossed around aboard a ship where the only good sense was imprisoned in the binnacle! Then there would be cause to complain along with my beloved Naso: *Derident stolidi verba latina Getae!*[98]

An English naval officer who heartily detested all learning was sitting in a tavern in London in the company of depressing examples of the same ilk. The conversation turned to a proposal that had been suggested for fixing longitude at sea by means of a timepiece. He mocked the idea for a while and then turned his attack on Euclid, astronomers and geographers. Even Newton was crazy. 'There sit the swots,' he shrieked so that the foam leaped out of all the beer mugs, 'there they sit by the fireside and want to teach you how to sail around the world. They promise you this and that, talk of new discoveries, new instruments and so on. But don't believe them. They imagine, for example, that the earth is round – *God damn their block heads!* I have travelled with Admiral Anson[99] from one end of it to the other and found it to be *by God, as flat as this table.*' If only this toad had been the only one of his kind in the world!

It would be ungrateful of me not to praise my fortunate situation in being on a ship where the two senior men both love and have knowledge. I am not so petty as to sing in a tone of craven flattery but I feel compelled to say for my own satisfaction that one of the two is just as much at home in the field of learning as the other is in the field of culture. There was no need for us to waste our tongues on worn-out stories of old East Indiamen, of compasses and weather and all the usual things. Our topics of conversation could rise from Linnaeus' plants to Descartes' vortices. We are at home with Hårleman, acquainted with Newton and not ashamed to be on friendly terms with Curtius and Virgil. How different from the usual circle of ship's officers! If Osbeck and Torén had been with us, we should not have had to read in their narratives how on this or that occasion their lack of freedom to go ashore prevented them from making scientific progress.

This can stand as a chapter on its own. I have glanced through it and find it to be closer to the truth than any so far.

Chapter XI

ARRIVAL AT THE CAPE.

Crebrescunt optatae aurae, portusque patescit- Virg.[100]

On the 15th of May we encountered the so-called Cape doves for the first time – birds that announce to the seafarer the vicinity of the Cape of Good Hope just as the arrival of the swallows at home is a presage of summer. On the 24th we were within the sandbanks and the following morning in sight of that high and famous Table Mountain.

This is the time of year when the winter months begin at the Cape and the usual anchorage in what is known as Table Bay is subjected to the most violent changes of weather. Ignorance of this cost the Portuguese the best part of a whole fleet in 1500 and was the cause of them moving on even though they were the first Europeans to have made a settlement there. We thus considered it inadvisable to enter the anchorage and, even though no Swedish vessel had been there before, we steered east instead round the headland to False Bay, some 30 miles from the town itself.

But passing the Cape without a storm is like passing Cadiz without the sores of love. No sooner were we congratulating ourselves on soon being ashore than a roaring horror of a wind hit us and set the whole of our Finnish principality into turmoil, all the more so since it very nearly blew away all our expectations of refreshment with it. For since it was blowing directly off the shore and we feared that it might continue for some time we were on the point of running before it and cancelling our visit. It began to moderate after some twelve hours, however, and out of consideration for the scorbutic condition of the sick aboard and in view of the great length of the journey from Norway to Java it was decided that we should take a short rest.

The following day the wind was favourable but as we veered into the bay it turned more and more against us so that we had to tack between the hills far into the night without reaching Simons Bay, the proper anchorage in normal circumstances. We were thus compelled to remain a little way out until the following day when it was once again possible to use eyes and sails.

The fourth mate was sent off in the jolly boat to reconnoitre the situation, caution being all the more necessary as we were navigating without a pilot among rocks in an unknown place and using inaccurate Dutch charts; they, like municipal lantern-men ashore, appear to be pointing out the right direction when in fact they are leading you astray. Deceived by the charts we steered farther up in the bay than we should have until we observed houses on one side, as well as a guard-ship that was anchored there. We immediately made a little swing to the left and let the anchor crash to the bottom while our purser fired a four-gun salute by way of greeting. The aforementioned guard-ship responded with eleven shots.

Chapter XII

WHICH HAS COST ME MORE EFFORT TO WRITE THAN IT WILL COST YOU TO READ.

- *Versus inopes rerum nugaeque canorae* – Horat.[101]

We had sailed from Norway to the land of the Hottentots in the space of eleven weeks. Anyone who knows the route may well say that we got there in double quick time. – The Dutch have settled in along these coasts and live very comfortably among the inlets that the effeminate Portuguese called *Promontoria Diaboli.*

The towering mountain ridges that surround False Bay on all sides inevitably attracted my poetic admiration, especially since *Finland* was the first Swedish ship ever to have lain among them. I saw them and began at once to grow big with young:

Ye oldest offspring of the earth, ye Table Mountain's kin,
Whose towering peaks reach heavenward into the ether thin,
Ye Afric's hills, unmoved, unsung, untouched through time
Though mighty ocean waves upon your foothills climb
And the cruel ruler of the winds roars past in chariot loud
Whipping his thund'rous chargers 'gainst your tops above the cloud -
Take to your bosom and your care these children of the north,
Protect them, calm them, rest them, e'er they once more set forth.
Salute now, tribe of Hottentots, the Swedish flag we wave,
Refreshment, peace and haven - no more than that we crave.
But should your minds contrariwise reject our honest plea
We've sixteen guns to put our case much more convincingly.
  Not for nothing do they call us
  Sons of Gustav, knights of Karl,
  For every race that tries to maul us
  Finds the chewing over hard.

Now on to you, Dutch sailors, who roam the oceans wide,
Whose lucky flag advances on an ever-rising tide,
Whose merchants with their tally books win land and fortunes more
Than ever Alexander could with all his arts of war.
Hear us, kindly merchants, who in these hills do dwell
In affluence so abundant you brew from grapes your ale,
Share just a little, please, with us - two thousand casks will do -
And while you're at it send us down of fruit a cart or two.
You won't find us on *Finland* grasping with our cash
Unlike the miser Dane or French and English trash,
For we are honest wights with honest Swedish ways
Who first of all our countrymen sail into this broad bay.

Geld, myne Heeren, Geld! [102] That's what you call empathy! I had scarcely uttered the word cash before we had Dutchmen aboard. – *De Posthoulder* or commander of the settlement, a Mr Kirst who was a Saxon by birth,came to visit us at once along with two others and invited the officers to dinner. We dressed and went ashore with an eight gun salute, using our new launch which had just been finished.

Chapter XIII

A QUICK GLANCE AT BOTH THE CAPE AND SWEDEN.

Nescio, qua natale solum dulcedine cunctos
Ducit et immemores non sinit esse sui. Ovid.[103]

The views in Norway were wretched, just as they were in this bay. The former had not struck me as strange as I had not expected anything better, but I was much put out by the latter since I had expected a Canaan. The high, threatening, treeless cliffs, overgrown with heather and half-covered with dry sand, could easily convince the stranger that he had landed up in Stony Araby. I had to bear in mind that it was winter in this country – which most resembles autumn at home even though the occasional snowdrift is to be seen on the mountain tops – and the country was not wearing its summer dress, but even that would do no more than alter the colour. Green grass, after all, is surely not the only pleasing feature of a country?

The human eye loves variety. I have travelled in Holland, France and England and nowhere have I enjoyed nature in such a variety of guises as in Sweden. At one moment there is a pleasant river winding its way between rocks and providing a source of power for all kinds of saws, mill wheels and hammers. Next there is a roaring waterfall plunging down from the rocky heights, then a quiet lake with fishing gear hanging on its shores and surrounded by fertile clearings and lush grazing land. On one side there is a smooth patch of arable land, on the other the murmur of the wind in a fine old spinney. If I descend into the vale I find an attractive alternation of small meadows, broad-leafed trees and ploughland. The hills that surround all this are decorated with evergreen pines and spruces, and even where the bedrock comes to the surface it is to a great extent cloaked in scrub and reveals itself in a hundred different forms with sloping strata, precipitous drops, hanging vaults, caves and the runnels created by streams. The eye of the traveller is never plagued by tedious monotony since he is quite likely to come across all this on one coaching stage. The hand of nature has given the surface of Sweden an uneven shape as if to provide us with a perpetual change of outlook. It is possible to travel for four hundred miles or more in France without coming upon a mountain, a precipice, a forest or a lake. The land is flat everywhere. What murderous monotony! In Sweden, however, no sooner are you up on a new hill than a whole new circle of prospects opens up. The roads may not be as comfortable as the French roads but they are worthy of admiration in that they are better than the hilly and difficult terrain would seem to allow. It might be slow work going uphill but rolling downhill is all the faster. – In short, the great architect has measured out our dwellings on the best piece of the whole globe. Precious homeland! Where will I find prettier summers? Where will I breathe healthier air? Where will I discover more blessings both above and below ground? We may not possess wine presses but we do have good barns of corn, and should a frozen foreigner with chattering teeth complain about our healthy winters he is forgetting that we have both wood as fuel and furs to clothe us; nor can he have tasted the incomparable pleasure of driving around the fields on shining ice or that of a glittering sleigh ride behind a snorting trotter with bells on its harness.

> Sweden, of all the Lord's creations
> Thou art to me most fine.
> For foreign shores no more I pine
> Since seeing other nations.

Those who from thee choose to roam
In search of daily fodder
Or knowledge fame and honour
Will find them more secure at home.

Traveller, remain where thou art born,
Plough with joy the homely furrow.
From journeys cometh nought but sorrow
And perhaps just a little le-learning.

What was I doing at the Cape? As if you can't see bare ravines closer to home! I did a little bit of travelling inland and it is full of long, bare mountain ridges still inhabited by tigers and lions however hard the Dutch have tried to eradicate them. Between the hills there are, admittedly, extensive and beautiful plains whose fertile loam rewards the labourer's efforts fifty-fold. But apart from the fact that the greater part of them still lie untouched and thus look wild, the two most splendid ornaments of nature – forests and rivers – are lacking here. Dutch industriousness has certainly tried to make good the lack of them by means of Art, by which I mean by constructing watercourses and planting trees, but this is only to be seen around their dwelling houses and is of little import. Thus, the Cape of Good Hope, where I had imagined I would find everything to be as extraordinary as its Constantia wine, possesses but few visible pleasures to the eye of the traveller. That's all I've been trying to say about the place.

Should you, however, visit the Dutchman at his country property you will find that there is health on his face, a pleasing neatness in his house and well-being in his vineyard. He resembles his European relations in habit, manner of thought and greed for money but is more hospitable than they are. He has moulded the patch of earth on which he has settled to his own taste and, when I consider the labour that he has invested in his cultivations, I think I recognize what Baron Holberg wrote about his forefathers back in the old country:

God created all the earth
Except the Netherlands.
The Dutch themselves, for what it's worth,
Made that with their own hands.[104]

The anchorage in Simons Bay was found to be both safer and more convenient than Table Bay and therefore Captain Ekeberg and our fourth mate Mr Ad.Burtz, by taking soundings and bearings as we entered and later by observations made from the height of the surrounding mountains, set about preparing accurate charts to prevent the difficulties that could be caused by the misleading information on older charts. These latter had very nearly led to the loss of an English ship on what they call Romans Rock.

On the 21st June we were once again ready to set sail and departed hence with a favourable wind.

Chapter XIV

A WORD TO CRITICS.

Gens inimica mihi Tyrrhenum navigat aequor. Virg.[105]

My dear fellows! Wisest of gentlemen! – What have you got against me? You're shrugging your shoulders. – What's that supposed to mean? I haven't written that badly, have I? – Perhaps you want me to address you in Latin? – All right. – *Miltiades, Cimonis filius, Atheniensis.* – [106] *Grammatica est ars loquendi et scribendi.* – [107] You're still not satisfied? – *O mihi trux pecudum genus!* [108]

I'll take your questions in order. – *I am a fool*, is that what you're saying first? – No harm in that, for fools usually succeed. I have studied the taste of the contemporary world and found that loveable idiocies are thought to be more pleasing than the very soundest wisdom: I am thus far too clever to be clever. Some authors are satisfied with the praise of a few connoisseurs and scorn the ignorant masses: in that case, let them write nothing but profound things. I, however, reckoning that safety lies in greater numbers, prefer to seek favour with the masses than with the few. Consequently, according to the natural ratio between those two kinds, I cannot write sensibly on more than one page in twenty.

Wisdom does not help anyone to get anywhere. You can see that from the case of the good, sound Leander. For all his good sense he courts Camilla in vain whereas that platitudinous prattler Powderpuff carries off the prize. Come with me and look at Erastus' collection of books: the volume of Reynard the Fox is absolutely worn out whereas the pages of Wolff [109]are still stuck together from the press. That is the taste of our age. When Cervantes wrote *Theologia moralis*,[110] no one read him; when Cervantes wrote *Don Quixote*, everyone read him. Caius had studied, went into the pulpit and could not get an audience. Caius took umbrage and went into the theatre where the whole world ran after him. Which are recited more often, the songs of Zion or those of Bellman? [111] – Now tell me where there is any advantage in not being a fool!

I am a slanderer, is that what you're saying now? – Fine, in that case we have the same profession so let's keep mum about each other. When did you ever hear of one exciseman betraying another or of one judge saying that another took bribes?

Anyway, who can be blamed if the truth is bitter? You are welcome to squeal if the shoe pinches! My pen, which is as honest as my heart, cannot call Granny's cat a tiger or Per Persson's ox a chamberlain. It would be nothing short of lunacy for me to praise that madcap Lisbetta for her chastity when she bears the evidence of her sin before her big as a regimental drum.

Censure what needs to be censured! It is perverse to blame the peacock for his feathers, but to praise him for his feet is even more so. So vice should not be protected, nor should virtue be attacked! Both are most easily distinguished when they are stamped with their appropriate trademarks.

I offend against all decency, I hear you continue. I am smutty and rude in, for instance, the chapter on vomiting and elsewhere. But, my fastidious Sirs, let us examine the concept of rudeness, for there is a great difference between a chancellor and a butler. Rudeness i-i-is rudeness – it's when someone is rude. – Oh woe, I'm afraid I can't defend myself! Help me, O great Donatus![112]

Well, *naturalia non sunt turpia.*[113] Am I supposed to call bell-bottoms bouquets and say that the sailor is manufacturing cream when he is actually spewing green bile? If I had referred to the twin reproductive organs of the shark as topgallant masts would you have understood what I meant? It's hardly my fault if our poor mother-tongue doesn't have any other word for *maitresse* than whore or if it compels me to render the Latin *politicus* as rogue. When your surgeon gives you an enema he politely asks you to turn your face up: is he really being polite? That's the sort of thing that I regard as exaggerated delicacy. It's a case of too much respectability leading to indecency.

It's quite another matter, however, where women are concerned. I am no more a defender of gross vulgarities than you are. That is forbidden territory or, at least, if you are going to lift the veil you should be fairly careful how you do it. Let me give you an example. A painter has no need to be ashamed of revealing Eve's bared breasts to your gaze but if he dares let his brush move down as far as her waist he has to hang a girdle of fig-leaves around her because now it is a case of *procul hinc, procul este, profani!*[114] I make exactly the same demands where Adam is concerned but if the foliage happens to be so loosely tied at the back that you catch a glimpse of his upper thigh I don't see any great need for us to be pernickety.

Apart from which, you lily-livered carpers, I always give a warning of the contents of each chapter in the few words I head it with. If I point out the bush that is covered with thorns it is clearly not my fault if you run into it and get pricked.

On the other hand, if the occasional unguarded blotch has dripped from my quill and brought a blush to the face of respectable womanhood I beg most humbly for forgiveness – not from you, gentlemen, but from the offended beauty. Her mirror will show her that the blemish she discovered on my page has been transformed into perfection on her face since a girl is never prettier than when a blush of modesty colours her cheeks. It is my hope, then, that she will forgive the vulgarity that escaped my hand seeing that it had such a beautiful result.

What else do you have to reproach me with? I am very puerile, I hear you say, and not in the least orthodox. To which my answer is that the former is the result of my age and health and, as far as the latter is concerned, I never promised you a collection of sermons.

You are doing me an injustice if you call me stupid, or witty, or learned. My trademark is *aliquid in omnibus* [115] and if you were to get to know me any better the whole work would be spoilt. We shall be doing each other a mutual service if we continue to remain unacquainted with one another.

You might, of course, reproach me with better reason for including so much about women in my worthless jottings – as if I were some effeminate petticoat pup. But everyone must know that these are the wares that sell best. You are never going to be left in the lurch with pretty wares of that sort even if you have shiploads of them; learned literature, on the other hand, will lie unasked for on the bookshelves like great piles of planks. So allow me to continue retailing my works undisturbed. Apart from which, I have a duty to please those of my friends present on the ship. Their usual question is: 'Have you got anything about girls?' When I answer no – as I did with this chapter – they go off with long faces and don't want to read what I've written.

The Third Finnish Expedition
From the Cape to Java

Chapter I

- – nautaeque per omne
Audaces mare qui currunt – – [116]

Seamen are migratory birds in perpetual motion, like the water upon which they sail. They often go to bed in one climatic zone and get up in another. The heat of the southern hemisphere holds no more terror for them than the cold of the North Pole. A grim and howling storm or a cheerful, gently murmuring, favourable wind is one and the same to them. They can endure anything.

The world is the seaman's homeland, the open air his abode, the sky his roof, the fishy realm his field. Not having a home, he is at home everywhere. Nature has no boundaries that he does not dare to cross and even the far-flung winds travel no farther than he does. From the far north of Europe he finds his way all the way down to the Antipodes. He greets the Japanese as countrymen and the Greenlanders as brothers. There is not a spot this side of the sun that is unknown to him. With the compass in one hand and the rudder in the other he rushes around the globe, drinks tea with the Chinese, buys meerkats in Java, gets drunk on Constantia wine among the Hottentots and coaxes the nugget of gold from the grasp of the stupid American in exchange for a jack-knife, a frying pan or a pathetic little mirror. He collects his taxes in all climes like some general revenue officer. He is there at every market like some pedlar from Västergötland. He knows all the oceans like a rorqual. In short, the sons of Neptune are the very soul of the whole of Creation.

Who is it who picks foreign flowers for the Linnés of Europe? He does. – Who brings home the silver from Peru and the gold from Chile? He does. – Who fetches rhubarb for ruined stomachs and cinchona bark for ague sufferers? He's the one. – How would His Excellency get the precious wines for his table and Her Grace a cup of mocha after her meal if the seaman wasn't daring enough to go for them? How would sweet Celinde get the chance to spread her wanton loveliness on a silken sofa or parade at the theatre in rich, gleaming fabrics if he did not seek out the land of the silkworms? And do you think that that proud and triumphant Corydon of Corydons would ever have usurped so many a heart if he had not fetched her diamonds from Hindustan to brighten the horizon of her brunette face? No, so you can thank the sons of Neptune for the lot! Columbus was a hero, Alexander just a butcher.

We were now at sea again. Table Mountain had already disappeared from view and the absence of the Cape of Good Hope was fairly easy to endure. The three weeks we had lain there was more than enough time to tire of the place. Even the winds seemed to feel the same way since for a full fortnight they blew so briskly that we were making 8 to 9 knots. With such good fortune in the sails and with bottles of Cape comfort in our cabins the hours passed easily.

My friends, who had not had the chance to travel outside False Bay, coaxed wine into me and the Cape out of me. I mean, they entertained me so liberally that I was compelled to describe to them everything I had seen, it being only the supercargo, the captain, the assistants, the ship's pastor and myself who had travelled there. I therefore append the following.

Chapter II

Per varios casus, per tot discrimina – Virg.[117]

Two days after our arrival in False Bay we set off on our journey to the Cape. I was told that we were travelling by land but as far as I could see we were travelling by sea for, apart from the showers of rain that gushed down on us, the breakers came so high that they overtopped the wheels every step of the way.

I was riding on an elderly and steady Rosinante and even had my Sancho Panza at my side. While I don't quite have the courage to compare myself with that incomparable knight Don Quixote, I can claim the honour of having spurred my way through rivers and seas like the bold soldiers of King Karl. The other gentlemen, packed into a large waggon that was covered with a piece of red, tarred sailcloth, were pulled along by five splendid pairs of horned oxen, the road being so difficult that horses could not be used. The coachmen must have been hired from Blåkulla;[118] I, anyway, have never seen blacker fellows depicted on the walls of old churches. They were two slaves from Madagascar.

Thus equipped we proceeded thirteen endless miles, sometimes down among the breakers along the bays, sometimes on the slopes of towering cliffs. The waggon preceded me and sometimes bounced sideways down the cliff so alarmingly that I began to dream of the sacrificial precipices of our ancestors. I suspected that the gentlemen were on the way to Valhalla rather than to the Cape and I recognized what good sense they had shown in taking the pastor along with them since if they had overturned on such steep slopes it would have been a case of burying rather than bandaging. They soon recognized this, and decided to trust to their own legs instead and to let the conveyance go in front. This was no more successful. Our travellers attempted to take a short cut, went astray and all of a sudden found themselves surrounded by water. What to do? It was too far to go back, too cold to swim and too boggy to ride. They sat down to take counsel and, the matter being sufficiently serious to demand a mixed court, even the blacks were called to join in. This time the latter proved to be more cunning than the whites. They investigated the depth with their long bamboo whips, squatted on their heels like monkeys, and indicated by means of grimaces that the gentlemen should mount on their shoulders. In this way they carried one of them after the other across the stretch of water. I cannot remember ever having laughed so much except for the time when I heard Dr. W. trying to prove that a widow could quite legitimately give birth to a baby fourteen months after the death of her husband. It crossed my mind that if a Swedish peasant had happened upon this scene he would have shaken at the knees, crossed himself a hundred times and opined that the devil was making off with us.

Wet and thoroughly shaken we arrived at noon at the relay station at Muisenburg where we found the new Company commissioner, Mr. La Fèvre, awaiting us *item* a better waggon, *item* a worse baker, and six horses from the Cape. The oxen were sent back. We ate a little and set off. Yet another sea to wade across! I have never been in a worse situation in my life. An overflow from the bay had created a lake right across our road and we had to cross it regardless of the cold squalls of rain that whistled round our ears. The waggon went first and managed to get through on its high wheels though the poor horses could scarcely keep their heads above water. But I, poor sinner that I am, had to follow, stretched out along the back of my Rosinante and more than once in danger of being washed overboard. It was impossible to steer a course with the reins because, since my hands were hanging in the horse's mane, I was carrying the reins in my mouth. There was consequently nothing I could do other than wriggle along using my two hind-paddles while trying to follow a bearing on what I took to be the waggon in front of me – which was floating along the surface like Noah's Ark.

But misfortunes never come in ones. While I was full of anxiety and contemplating the window of Heaven above me and the waters of the abyss below,[119] the baker – fat bag of flour that he was – sat there keeping the conversation going at my expense. He watched as I heaved my body, now to starboard, now to port, in the throes of my agony. He feared that the current might take me and he asked the gentlemen whether they had had me insured in Amsterdam. When he noticed the squalls of rain gushing along my back, he said with a sigh: *Der Himmel schwitzt.*[120] And when he noted a wave that hit me broadside, he voiced the opinion that, as a faithful Lutheran, I need have no fear since it is possible to walk on water etc. as long as one has just a crumb of faith no larger than a peppercorn.[121] Meanwhile, I had to lie in silence and listen to the distressing echo of the others' mirth from the waggon. In my anxiety, however, I was more intent on salvation than vengeance and, in any case, I couldn't get close to Mr Flourbag because of the wet weather. But I do remember that I wished I could have hanged him on the tail of my post-horse.

It is, however, not written in my stars that I am to drown. Finally and triumphantly I rode up onto the far shore, though I came near to imitating the Pope [122] who, during His Holiness' entry to Rome the year before, had been thrown from his horse even though his noble cardinals – those worthy pillars of the church – were supporting him at the sides. The reason being that my uncouth Rosinante had no sooner stepped out of the sea than, simultaneously peeing and snorting, she began to shake the water out of her coat so pitifully that I lurched this way and that in the saddle, all the time becoming more worried since she showed signs of wanting to roll over. We eventually made friends again and continued our journey. The road was reasonably good for the remaining twenty miles but the excessive rain had made it so slippery that I still don't understand how my head is sitting on an unbroken neck. My jade tripped over several times but without taking me with her more than once, which was when she sat down on her hindquarters like a monkey and caused me to fall off backwards.

At 5 o'clock in the afternoon we arrived in Cape Town, its white houses and black roofs appearing from a distance like a large, scattered flock of sheep grazing at the foot of Table Mountain. We were all accommodated at the house of the aforementioned Mr. La Fèvre. I have nothing to say about this journey apart from what Dalin said about pepper: 'that's a spice that I'll never forget.'[123]

Chapter III

NOT TO BE READ BY THOSE WHO WANT TO LAUGH

- – *Nil non mortale tenemus* – Ovid.[124]

Half an hour after our arrival the Vice-Governor of the Cape was buried. The cortège was a large one. The militia marched in front with lowered pikes and suitable funeral music. Behind them came men bearing wreaths on poles and a man with the arms and insignia of the deceased. Next came the corpse and the highest ranking men of the place accompanied by a long black column of the less elevated citizenry.

The graveyard lies a short distance outside the town. I followed the throng there and was more than a little put out when I saw such a mass of people walk up to the grave only to turn back immediately without offering up a single word of prayer. They broke up just as if they were leaving a bourse. No earth was scattered on the dead man by a priest even though there were three of them present: they simply had a couple of slaves shovel the grave full and that was that. I was upset to see a man of rank being buried like a horse and it could not fail to confirm me in my Lutheranism, which I venerated as a wise middle course between the too much of Catholicism and the too little of the reformed churches.

This depressing sight, along with my own unpleasant journey, brought a cloud to my face and thoughts of death to my soul. It was not without a shudder that I imagined our final great step. The footsteps of misfortune were visible in all things and nowhere could I find those of happiness. We chase around the world in search of wealth and in the end our gains amount to no more than three shovels full of earth. Today we are the rulers of half of mighty Africa, tomorrow we shall own no more than a little six-foot hole there.

– - *quis talia fando,*
Temperet a lacrymis! – Virg.[125]

Whate'er thy worldly gain
'Twill ever be in vain:
Upon this earth there are no joys.
Look rather to the tomb
Where thy bones will come:
Crutch and sceptre equally are toys.

Adrift on a treach'rous wave
Sails pleasure's lustful slave
In the gilded yacht of desire.
Fools trust that lucre's might
Can purchase rank and right:
Croesus and Irus alike will both expire.[126]

Vain the victory in strife
That crowns the hero's life:
Death spreads o'er him its cloaking shroud.
Interred in Russian soil
For all their warrior toil
Lie Swedish conquerors proud.

Is beauty not immortal?
No, at winter's portal
Nettles die and roses too.
The light of wisdom, then?
No, Death's unpitying pen
Strikes through both Maevius and Maro.[127]

Even virtue cannot save
Us from the claws of age.
Innocence herself is not reprieved.
Not e'en an eagle's flight
Will outpace th' eternal night
In which we are by Death received.

O miserable mortal man
Who seek where'er you can
A firm foundation for your stay:
Might and glory time will rust,
Gold and wealth become but dust -
They promise joy then fade away.

The miser with his savings
And penny-pinching cravings,
He too in death will pay his turn.
Will wealth and worldly status
Have any power to sate us
When we are prey unto the worm?

Most blessed of us all
Is he whose needs are small
And whose modest pleasures match them.
Whate'er heights we ascend
The tomb lurks at the end
As the hub of our ambition.

Chapter IV

ODDMENTS CONCERNING CAPE TOWN

Quicquid venerit obvium loquamur – Mart.[128]

This will not be a description, merely some remarks. I shall depict things as they appear to my eyes not as others find them. So it is quite likely that my opinions will not be approved of by everyone. The reason why travellers furnish differing accounts of one and the same thing is not so much a matter of the particular time that they visited a place as of their individual ways of perceiving things. One traveller may be of the opinion that the Cape of Good Hope is the prettiest dwelling place on the globe; someone else calls it a barren and unpleasant wasteland. Both are right – as long as they add that

that is how it seems to them. Some people consider the Chinese to be the wisest, most powerful and blissful of all races. Others, however, say that they are cowardly wretches, lacking decent habits, freedom and knowledge. Neither of the two is telling a lie as long as they admit that that is their opinion, there being good reason on both sides.

Two travel writers may thus differ in their judgments concerning what is beautiful and what is ugly without offending against historical truth. Were Caius to say that the inhabitants of Madagascar are white and Titus, on the other hand, to insist that they are black, one of them must inevitably be lying. Were Caius, however, to praise them as being pious and Titus to accuse them of being brutal, both of them could be right since moral features have a hundred aspects whereas natural features only have one. If our critics ashore were kind enough to bear this in mind they would no longer cast slurs upon our honour by referring to us undeservedly as gross liars.

Since I tend to note down what amuses me rather than what may be of profit to others I have no desire to sneak my papers in among the travel narratives of learned men, but justice demands that I take sides with them against ignorant critics. The likes of Osbeck, Torén and the rest of them go to great trouble to acquaint us with foreign parts. Am I to keep quiet when I hear their names being mocked by blockheads?

I shall not bother to defend myself. Others may judge as they wish, so long as I am permitted to cut my own quill! My views of the Cape are as follows:

I am not concerned with a description of the town but, to the credit of the inhabitants, I must admit that they are very courteous to foreigners – far more so than they are to their own European countrymen. They speak very highly indeed of Swedes, for which reason I must acknowledge publicly those members of my nation who have been there before us: what, if not their honest behaviour, could have given rise to it? The French, however, are in bad odour among them because of their indulgent capers with the womenfolk and the Danes have left plenty of smutty stories behind them too.

Apart from that a foreigner with some small ability to converse with them can knock on any door and be welcome everywhere. I have tried it myself. Unknown and without introduction I relied on my Swedish face and was well received everywhere. If you accompany them out of town to their country residences you will never be allowed to leave until you have perambulated their wine cellars barrel by barrel and drunk a glass of each sort. You will make them genuinely sorry if you don't call on them once a day.

The governor, Baron Tullbagh, whose long service has won him a well-deserved reward in that he has risen from being a mere soldier to be the leading man in the country, is an elderly and respected gentleman. It is not only by the Dutch that his name deserves to be held dear for, apart from the courtesy that he has shown to Swedes in general, he has performed valuable services in the scientific field for Linné, which is why there are many plants bearing the grateful name *Tulbaghia* to be found in the latter's papers.[129]

The fiscal (Baron von Plettenberg), Secretary van der Berg (descended from a Swedish grandfather) and Supercargo Hemmy, all three of them members of the government, as well as Major Du Prene, also deserve mention as being special friends to our nation.

Here you will meet three kinds of faces apart from white ones: yellowish-brown Hottentots, pitch-black slaves and coloured mongrels, that is the extra-marital offspring of a European and his black *demoiselle*. The whole lot are heathens.

Hottentots, the natural inhabitants of the country, are considered to be free fellow nationals and can even become citizens of the Cape if they adopt Christianity. Most of them, however, have retreated from the Cape itself back into the mountainous district and prefer to retain the wild style of life of their forefathers rather than imitate the artificial customs of the Europeans. The Dutch are very eager to convert them and they therefore pay the full wages of a deacon who carries out missionary work among them. In spite of this costly effort the Hottentots still prefer their ancient heathen darkness. They are supposed to be unutterably filthy, but I have been informed that the account given in a number of German travel narratives that their holy men or sacrificial priests spray sanctity around them with their own water at weddings and funerals is an invention.

Slaves, mainly bought on Madagascar, are the most valuable possessions the inhabitants have. When property is transferred they go with it just like any other livestock. They perform all the tasks, indoors as well as outdoors, since the woman of the house and her daughters sit as if rooted to the tea table and do nothing. The slave race is smallish and weak-limbed. I have seen four of them gathered around a load that a single one of our lads from Dalarna would have thrown onto his shoulder – the slaves included. I think this can be traced to their improper intercourse, for both sexes are thrown together in a camp and they couple randomly like mindless animals, often at as young an age as twelve or thirteen. The way their masters leave them to their worthless heathendom is indefensible. There's the Dutch conscience for you! If there is to be any healthy breeding then a European has to be involved. It is for this reason that a host considers it a great courtesy to his humble house if a guest happens to become enamoured of a black-eyed maiden, for anyone who enlarges his slave girls is also enlarging his wealth. An Englishman will occasionally take *a dear black sweetheart*, and an urbane Frenchman does not miss the chance of throwing himself *aux pieds de sa belle brune*.[130] My own innocent countrymen, however, generally consider this to be bestiality.

Which do you think is blacker: her skin or their deeds?

You will find speakers of all kinds of languages among the whites. The militia, in particular, bears witness to the flourishing white slave trade in Amsterdam. There are hundreds of debt-ridden wretches serving as soldiers here and bewailing their lecherous youth. The Dutch are amazing! There is nothing that is useless to them. They carry on a trade in Christian souls in Europe and among the Japanese they accept enamelled ornaments in exchange for their expressions of faith. They know how to convert everything into money – even our Lord's rain – for if you go to the Herring Tower in Amsterdam you will come across six or eight yachts built solely for the trade in water. Not to mention the fact that every shower that passes over their roofs has to pay its dues since they have had lead-lined balconies erected on top of their houses to retain the rain. I remember having read about a Dutchman who, during the war against Louis XIV, was asked how he dared trade with the enemy. 'Myn Heer,' he answered, 'if there was any profit to be made in Hell I would take the risk of singeing my sails there too.'

A number of French refugees were accepted here after the Revocation of the Edict of Nantes [131] and they now live in a princely fashion in the valleys inland. Their women are the most renowned beauties at this end of Africa.

Germans make up half the population of the Cape and they are Lutherans. They collected funds for the building of a church of their own long ago but have not been able to get permission to proceed with it. An incomprehensible policy on the part of a trading government! This is why they always inquire after Lutheran pastors whenever ships arrive, and on this occasion our chaplain agreed to give them communion and preach to them in their own language. Which he did, and received a collection of 50 riksdaler for doing so.[132]

There is only one church in the town and four out in the country. The company pays the wages of three pastors at the former and each of the latter has one. Their income is so generous that being a pastor and being rich may be considered as one and the same thing. Here, just as in Holland, they are all equal – there being no distinctions of rank in the spiritual estate.

As far as my eye can tell the town is as big as Gothenburg but neither so densely populated nor so populous. The number of inhabitants is said not to exceed six thousand. Better class people speak French and some know English. Dutch and German are the main languages.

Chapter V

CONTINUATION

- Eadem non omnia Tellus - Ovid.[133]

The garden at the Cape is worthy of the attention of plant lovers as well as of husbandmen. It is a joy to see how the energetic Dutch have had the skill to create a union between what is useful and what is pleasing. On the one hand it provides a sufficiency of all kinds of vegetables for the visiting ships of the Company as well as for a large part of the town, while on the other hand it offers the curious naturalist a rich storehouse of rare plants from the four corners of the world. If it is fruit you love, you will find the most select varieties here. If you enjoy strolling, nothing could be more pleasurable. I could only look with wonder at the mighty, intractable oaks that had been disciplined into obedient hedges and artful, covered pathways. French gardens, especially those that have been cultivated by the famous hand of Le Nôtre,[134] possess more, and more diverse, ornamentation but fewer fundamental advantages. They seem made for the eye alone whereas this garden is capable of appealing to all five senses. The zoo that is attached to it provides the visitor with a pleasant diversion to his contemplations, for it contains a strange collection of living rarities. The ostriches and a bird called the secretary bird were what amused me most.

But, apart from this garden for strolling in, the Cape has nothing else to offer in the way of public pleasures. The theatre, opera and masquerade are not even known here by name and, what seems even more incomprehensible, there is no tavern, coffee-house, billiard room or discussion club either. I exclude a couple of low pubs for sailors. All of this gives the place the appearance of a desert to anyone who has come from gay, crowded Europe. After two days everything is old hat. Surrounded by such depressing monotony you feel empty and begin to get bored, and if you want more than mere eating and drinking you won't enjoy yourself for long here. The meagre topics of social intercourse, formulated in outworn and everyday phrasing or restricted to a tedious cycle of gossip, make it impossible for a foreigner to initiate a gallant and polite conversation. The word hoard of the Dutchman is far too poor for that. When I pay *Myn Heer* a visit it will be the same thing today and tomorrow: smoke a pipe and have a drink! If I'm bold enough to approach *Mefrowe* - lame chair-cover that she is as she sits there with her hands crossed and her unused legs resting on a warming-pan since idleness always feels the cold – she will whine her eternal *koppie the, Myn Heer*![135] And when I accept it she will pass me a piece of sugar candy, hard as flint and as small as the pupil of her eye, which I shall have to use both for that cup and for the three following ones in accordance with her own thrifty example of courtesy. If she offers me coffee it will be as unadorned as her tea. Should I say some pretty words to her she will answer with a platitude or call for a spittoon. Should I have a nice little box or any other pretty trinket with me she will request with tasteless boldness to be allowed to see it, then she will smile with envious eyes as she turns it between her fingers while expressing a wish that she possessed one like it. She is even capable of stuffing it into the pocket of her gown and laughing, as though her gracious grimaces might be sufficient recompense for me. In short, the womenfolk were the most insufferable aspect of the Cape, which is why I preferred to stick in the men's corner where I could at least hide my dissatisfied face in a billowing cloud of canaster smoke.

The Dutchman is very ceremonious without being in the least civilized. Pipe in mouth and wearing a hat that seems to swallow rather than cover his unbrushed head, he is to be found uttering a whole mass of French compliments in the midst of a circle of women. The smoke that billows in great and ever-widening squirls from the corners of his mouth might easily convince you that he is laying siege to the fair sex with twelve-pounder cannon, and were it not that their sparkling eyes illuminated the darkened horizon like the stars at night you would need to feel your way forward with your hands. At table he accompanies every mouthful with a courtesy and it is impossible to empty a glass without a stream of well-intentioned Good Healths. You will never see him spit on the floor, nor will he either come to the table or leave it without washing. You should, however, not be put out when he self-indulgently throws his legs up on a chair or belches in your face a couple of times. Ceremonious peasants!

The courses they eat at table are like Voltaire's ideas – showy but lacking in substance. Four Swedish courses provide more nourishment than eighteen of theirs since they consist mainly of fruit and vegetables. These finally become as monotonous to the palate as their polite mealtime phrases become to the ear: *Smaakelick eeten, Inclinatie, Gesondheit* and so on.[136]

It amuses me to recall Baron Holberg: 'Dutch houses,' he says, 'are filthy in the midst of all their cleanliness because, while they do not spit on the floor, they fill the tables with spittoons.'[137] What Oxenstierna says about Holland is just as neat: *C'est un pays, òu le démon de l'or est couronné de tabac, assis sur un trône de fromage.*[138]

Chapter VI

A DISSERTATION ON BEAUTIES

Ingenium movit sola Corinna meum – Ovid.[139]

The pleasures of novelty are delightful. The sons of Neptune, tossed for so long on the watery realm, come ashore and imagine they will find an angel in every skirt. Many was the Alack and Alas sighed on these shores on our arrival! In my imagination I can still hear them echoing from the rocky but sympathetic ravines. Poor lads! They didn't need to see more than the shadow of a female body to be entranced and I should feel sorry for them if I didn't know that they could cool down just as easily as they were kindled.

Cape girls are pretty but they are still not goddesses. They have the advantage over others of never being scarred by the smallpox since that does not occur here except when occasionally introduced by a foreign vessel. That was how a Danish ship ten years ago reduced the population of the town by two thousand souls. But the contagion has never proved able to spread inland, whither the people move on such occasions. Given a European upbringing and more intercourse with the cultivated world the girls could become perfect women but, lacking these, they remain no more than pretty-pretty country dolls. They have a blooming complexion but this, for the most part, lasts such a short time that those who were beautiful last year are ugly this. Brought up to do nothing, rough and lacking urbanity, they become plain housewives, just as their daughters do after them. To compare them with our girls, particularly those in Sweden, would be to show them in a very bad light.

I have observed the women of many nations on my travels and I have looked at them with an observant eye. I have never had much luck with Swedish girls so it cannot be out of gratitude that I support them. Nevertheless, justice compels me to give them precedence over all the rest in the matter of beauty – as long as we are talking in general, of course.

> Ah, beauties of sweet Swedish womanhood, I swear
> That those whose lowly taste and mole-eyed vision dare
> To claim that you have rivals in this mortal round
> Deserve the cuckold's horns upon their foolish brow.
> Your skin, blessed by the pure northern sky,
> Is like some flowery field where rose and lily vie.
> Nature, abundant, gave all and left her store deplete
> To furnish you with beauty and with disposition sweet.
> Were altars still constructed in praise of women's grace,
> To none but Swedish womanhood would I a candle place.
> In search of female beauty I have voyaged far and wide
> But I found it to perfection on the homecoming tide.
> Yes, English maids are pretty when they fire Cupid's dart
> But the snowy whiteness of the face is mirrored in the heart.
> A snow-white cheek by blood unwarmed, by blush unstained,
> Reveals the lack of fire coursing through the veins.
> The *jolie* girls of France, however finely painted,
> Rely o'er much on brushwork that leaves Nature's efforts tainted.

With rouge and powder wiped away there's nought to justify
The beauty you imagined when you viewed with distant eye.
The further south you travel, the less the female vigour,
And as the body loses strength, the foolishness grows bigger.
A touch alone destroys the flower, soon their bloom has fled,
Sufficient to adventure but not to wifely bed.
Here I number every maid
Who blooms along the Cape Town shore.
Sweet the flowers she puts forth
For a season e'er they fade.
Transient beauty has its pleasure
But I, who seek a loving wife
To be my company for life,
Will look elsewhere at leisure.

Were I allowed to choose a whole harem as the Turks do I would do my choosing here but, compelled to be satisfied with one, I demand more durable wares. These girls will scarcely endure one childbed before their blossom withers.

Chapter VII

CONCERNING MUSICAL MADEMOISELLES

Saxa ferasque lyra duxit – -[140]

Apart from virtue there is nothing that better suits the fair sex than music. This accomplishment should be theirs alone. It occupies the angels of Heaven, so why not those of Earth as well? Nature seems to have designed them for it. For what other purpose would they possess such nimble little fingers and such a flexible and delightful voice were they not for trilling a pastoral song at the piano? They possess a more delicate skin than the male and with it they have finer feelings, are better able to accept impressions of tenderness, daintiness and delight. The whole of their physical structure is musical.

Consider the shapely Clorinde: is there not sweet harmony in her figure? You will find nothing but pure accord from head right down to little playful foot. A pair of fiery eyes that are in pretty agreement with their two finely drawn eyebrows, a rounded forehead that perfectly matches her plump cheeks, smiling rosy lips, a neat chin, throat, breast, hand – one after the other they reveal the sweetest harmony. The whole figure is a living concert. The pipes of an organ and the strings of a fiddle are not in better tune. Is there anyone who cannot see that Nature intended the fair sex to be musicians? The piano, the lute, the flute should be their subjects. The bassoon, the drum and the trumpet are for the stronger male.

Think of the advantages that would accrue to good society from this! Think how many less civilized pastimes could be dispensed with! There is that madcap Jocosa who skitters around the town either frittering away her husband's fortune at balls and playhouses or tittle-tattling away the honour of her fellows during evenings of gossip. The quiet Sappho, on the other hand, disturbs nothing but her keyboard. With a heart as merry as her music she finds joy without seeking it on other people's doorsteps and when you hear her, alone or in a circle of chosen friends, urging from the clavichord all the sweet amiability that lies within herself, you would believe that you are seeing an angel in human guise.

Orpheus could move stones. He tamed tigers and Cerberuses with his lute. And many is the young Sappho who has a Cerberus for a husband! He comes home in the evening sullen, surly and stamping. She meets him with smiling eyes – it has no effect. She plucks a mournful note on the lute-string – it helps, the ice begins to soften. His harsh brow loses one furrow after the other and before he has managed to undress she has turned her tiger into the most docile of lambs. He gets into bed as merry as an allegro. Modest Sappho follows him and fastens the bed-curtains with a pin.

I am making these observations in memory of a pleasant evening we had at the home of *Myn Heer* Hemmy at the Cape. His daughters were competent musicians and the elder, in particular, excelled. They had heard that our supercargo was reputed to be a great musician and they longed to compete with him. He came and he brought joy with him on his fingertips. The first test took place on a sweet little organ. The girls opened the game and seized the admiration of all present. They then obliged the aforementioned supercargo to take his seat, thinking to surprise him with their most difficult sheet of music, but their trick came to nothing. Whatever advantage their brown and pretty eyes won over him was lost on this occasion to his nimble fingers. They admitted as much themselves, however much he tried to convince them of the opposite.

The music now shifted to the clavichord, at which they likewise competed for precedence. In the meantime, however, the sound of a harp could be heard from the hallway. I desired to see the David who could pluck such sweet notes. I went thither and he was such an abomination that my hair stood on end under my wig. There stood a shaggy black virtuoso from Blåkulla – a slave from Batavia [141] – with not a touch of white visible apart from the two dozen grinning teeth. The girls had placed him there, as if lying in ambush for our attentive ears. This lovable demon was brought in to accompany the elder mademoiselle and it turned into a divine concert for she could also sing. Never have I seen more joy on my captain's face. He liked the black musician better than I liked the white and no one can deny that he was a skilful devil. To watch this ruffian with his ten pitch-black claws plucking the sweetest harmonies from the strings, sometimes in a rolling forte, sometimes in a dying piano, at the same time as watching her fly all around the keys, begin a pretty trill with her lips and continue it with her finger while slowly moving her eyes in a way that expressed all the tenderness that was in the music itself – all this was a performance that left me uncertain whether it was my eyes or my ears that were revelling in it more.

The third round was played out on a cither, on which the same mademoiselle strummed with a quill the chords of a pastoral song she was singing. We devoured her with our eyes. The girl was no more than ordinarily beautiful but the music endowed her with attractions that a mere beauty can never possess. Her finger touched the string, the string produced a note, the note went right to the heart and the heart shone in our eyes. There was such sweet accord in all her limbs, and when I add that she was one of the richest lasses at the Cape you will understand that she was just as well tuned for the marriage bed. I can never recall that evening without murmuring the motto of the Amarant Order: *Dolce nella memoria.*[142]

Chapter VIII

A BITTER PILL FOR MY COUNTRYMEN

Respue quod non es – - Horat.[143]

The Swedes ape others from simple civility, just as the Germans and the Danes do. In London we let our forelocks hang down over our foreheads, in Paris we go round with our hats under our arms, in Amsterdam we wear huge trousers. We follow the simple principle: 'Stick your finger in the ground and smell which country you are in.' We thus adopt all the customs – even the most preposterous – of the places to which we have come.

This exaggerated courtesy is worthy of ridicule. No one denies that a stranger enjoying protection in a foreign land should be subject to whatever laws its current politics dictate. But this obligation does not extend to customs, clothes and habits of thought. Am I to be ashamed of reading at table just because the Englishman does not do so? Am I to take the flour from my mouth and powder my hair with it just because the vain Frenchie has that custom? Should our skippers lift a leg and break wind just to accommodate themselves to some coarse Dutchman? That is no different from telling me: 'When you get to Java you must squat on your haunches and chew betel nut. When you are in Russia you must eat garlic and drink yourself silly.'

I can quite easily eat my fill without a *Smaakelick eeten*. Nor does a Swede need to pump himself full of disease just because a Dutchman says *Gesondheit*. Does it do me any credit to sit with my pipe in my mouth and my hat on my head in a circle of ladies just because such behaviour is thought proper by Cape gallants? No! I shall not even adopt their most courteous custom, which is to salute the fair sex with a triple kiss when they are coming or going, for just imagine how many moss-covered, trembling old wifie's cheeks that would add up to! While kissing them you would be afraid that one of their rotten teeth would fasten in your lip, or that one of the facial furrows would be passed on to you by the contact – not to mention the risk you run of causing her rickety nose to list. And as far as the younger ones are concerned this custom entails no more than a lifeless proximation of skin without either fire of force. Give me a kiss in Sweden any day! I seldom get one but when I do I feel it right down to my big toe.

My countrymen would thus be well advised to stick loyally to the customs of their homeland, especially since these are a sensible middle course between the excessive ceremoniousness of the French and the vulgar bluntness of the Dutch. An Englishman remains an Englishman wherever he goes and why shouldn't we do likewise? If I live as I am used to living my manners will be easy, unforced and natural. If I depart from that way I shall be about as successful as a monkey in a long wig. Would *Myne Heeren* deny us the same services as they provide now? Of course not – because they are not likely to stop loving pieces of eight! We are already showing them too much courtesy by speaking their language since they never learn ours in return. I, for my small part, have determined to be a Swede everywhere.

The Sunday after Whitsun we were all ready to return to the ship in False Bay but a violent attack of colic confined our supercargo to his bed and caused some days' delay. The second assistant supercargo and myself, however, set off in advance. The conveyance cost twelve riksdaler for the same distance as I should have been able to travel for a third of the price in Sweden. That's how shameless the Dutch can be when they get the chance. The cost of wagons is largely to blame for this since an ordinary wicker cart can cost as much as 400 riksdaler, but the charge for hiring one is nevertheless utterly excessive.

We visited a number of beautiful farms on our way and happy faces met us everywhere. The people who live in the country are satisfied to be known by the honest name of farmer though they dress like townsmen and live like noblemen. Contentment and abundance flourish around their dwellings and all beverages and foodstuffs are consequently available at a very low price. We travelled very close to Constantia where they press what are probably the most delicious wines in the world. It is situated at the foot of a long ridge of mountains that protect the vineyards from east winds and that, along with the character of the soil itself, is said to be the reason why this particular grape does not occur in other places even though attempts have been made to spread it. Unsuccessfully, however.

Towards evening we arrived at Commandant Kirst's house at the bay and there we found those of our companions who had remained behind fully occupied in dancing with the girls of the place, as I shall report in the next chapter.

Chapter IX

- – *Spelmanni gnidite gigis* – [144]

How now, Brothers! You're making good use of your feet! All this stamping can be heard thundering a couple of miles away. You had me pretty well convinced that the rocks themselves were dancing since I could hear them keeping time with you. – Let's have a look at these nymphs of yours, and I'll let you know what I think of them.

Is this the commandant's daughter *Gessie*? She is a pretty child, pink as the dawn sky, fiery and free. Watch when she smiles and see the mischief gleaming from her eyes and from the pretty little dimples in her cheeks. – Ugh! Now she's roaring with laughter and that doesn't suit her. It makes the whole little idol of flesh shake so horrendously that you can feel the vibrations in the boards she is standing on. Her face presents me with a picture of sensual pleasure but lacks the elevated and refined quality that can command an observer's respect. I must thus include her among those beauties who are better able to win a heart than to retain it. And the dancing master who didn't put her undercarriage in better shape should be ashamed of himself: you can see, can't you, that she walks with turned-in toes like a goose. Nor are her mannerisms very polite. – All right, all right, gentlemen! Don't get in a huff! I'm just giving you my opinion. You are welcome to call her a goddess if you want to.

Now who is that little girl with the big blue eyes?

– The wealthy *Miss Hörter* from the Cape. – D..n me if she isn't the most regular beauty I've seen in this country! What a pretty shape and attached to an even prettier face! I must study her for a while. – Do you know what I think, gentlemen? She is so beautiful that she is ugly. She is a flower without scent or, more accurately, a beautiful picture that catches the eye without touching the heart. Gessie with her small faults is more pleasing. That's the way it is. Nature is never less successful in her creations than when she uses circles and measuring gauges. I'm the same in that respect for I don't write too badly except when I'm trying to do it really well.

Now the tall Miss standing there by the Dutch skipper and fanning away the tobacco smoke with her handkerchief, who is she? – *Miss Aletta*, cousin of the last girl. – Now there's a twelve-pounder! Do you know what she seems like to me? Like Cape sheep, which carry most of their weight at the tail-end and are better at filling the pot than satisfying the taste buds. Poor lass! Not ugly, but with too much of the worthy matron about her to be called a pretty girl.

These three sweethearts were actually the ornaments of the ball. It was a pleasure to watch them stepping out on their turned-in feet in a series of contradances and prancing their posteriors backwards and forwards while our Swedish lads crossed and recrossed their legs and beat time on their knees opposite them. The former had no understanding of dancing beyond the actual movements and the latter still had their sealegs. In spite of that, our boys put the Dutch completely in the shade, there being also present at the dance the officers of a ship bound for Batavia from Amsterdam that had arrived in the bay along with us. They just sat forgotten in a corner while our young fellows, fussing like bees around flowers, kept up a boisterous shindig with the nymphs and enjoyed a clear advantage.

I have noticed in various places that my countrymen are lucky with foreign women. The French, so the women say, are far too saucy and thin-legged; the English have more flesh on them but are sullen and importunate; but the Swede, according to the prettiest sources, unites the courtesy of the former and the build of the latter in one person. What delightful flattery from pretty lips! Gratitude compels me to admit that they themselves are as pretty as angels for how can I call people ugly when they say that I am beautiful?

In this manner we held a ball every evening. One strange thing I noticed was that those of our company who were married were allowed most indulgence by the girls whereas the bachelors had more or less to fight for whatever advantages they got. A stupid policy! As if experience cannot exist outside the married state! In the end this had the effect that even the unshaven lads were swearing that they had wives, children and chattels in order to increase their credit.

The supercargo, the first assistant and Commissioner La Fèvre arrived from the Cape on the following Friday. The dancing continued on that evening too but the aforementioned gentlemen and our captain considered the settling of accounts more urgent and they were cruel enough to give the curtseying nymphs a stern refusal when they were invited to join in the pleasures. This could hardly fail to provoke the girls, who now put their heads together and came up with a plan of revenge that brought them complete success. They had the number of fiddles doubled, dragged out onto the floor everyone who had life and breath, and romped, warbled and stamped reels so spiritedly that the pens were shaken out of the hands of the sitting officers. You would have thought there was an earthquake in the house. Chairs, benches and tables seemed to come to life in order to support their intentions. The supercargo, who was supposed to be doing calculations, accidentally mixed numbers and musical notation in the confusion. The captain was trying to sketch the cliffs that surround the bay but all of his cliffs failed. The first of his cliffs was as long as a bass-viol, the second as round as a starched petticoat and the third just like a woman's shoe. A strong gust of wind caused by Aletta's gown swinging past knocked everything over – including the inkwell – and totally extinguished all the candles in that corner. Poor La Fevre was still trying to put pen to paper but his hand seemed to be keeping time with the girls' feet. He put his fingers in his ears, he stamped, he begged, he swore. Nothing helped. He moved away to another corner. The dance followed him there. He lighted his pipe to smoke the bees away. All in vain. The poor fellow finally became so confused that when he came to read out his bill and say a hundred riksdaler for sheep, a hundred for goats, capons, lemons etc. it came out as a hundred riksdaler for fiddlers, ditto for contradances, so much for strings and so on. In short, our vengeful Amazons would pay no heed to any conditions for peace short of the unconditional surrender of the fortress. The enemy were finally compelled to march out from behind the rampart of writing tables, their arsenal of inkwells, sand boxes and pens was abandoned and they themselves were led in triumph through the streets in the form of a long contradance. It was a joy to see our elderly captain running neck and neck with the similarly elderly Mrs Kirst, and even more of a pleasure to see the poor commissioner forced into the chase in the merciless grip of Aletta until his tongue was hanging out. The supercargo, being indisposed, escaped but all the others had to spend the whole night dancing along beneath the rows of ladies' handkerchiefs.

Chapter X

USEFUL READING FOR ALL SEAFARING GALLANTS

Speluncam Dido dux et Trojanus eandem Deveniunt – – Virg.[145]

I shall never forget how, like some second Actaeon, I happened upon a Diana that very evening. It was my intention to go outside and – well, count the Seven Stars – when I heard an unknown voice whispering hastily behind the porch door: *O! my dear, my dear!* Curiosity enticed me to lie in ambush. I put my ear to the door and picked up snatches of a declaration of love that must be among the nicest of its kind.

Since the door could not shield them completely from the envious gaze of the moon I noticed the protruding corner of a woman's gown, but who the Damon was I had no wish to find out. But I do remember that he sighed a word of Swedish, a word of English, a word of Dutch and so on. – *Charming creature – Ich liuge nicht – Ich love ye, with all min hart – give me a kuss for min hund – my dear.* – Here there was a short pause and it sounded as if two people were about to kiss. I listened further and heard a second, more delicate voice: *Ah! myn Heer, gey beent een schelm – de Ostindische lievde is niet veel te vertrauwen – go! go! niet mehr – Ik hebb ge twee gegeeven.* – The other, however, did not seem to be minded to leave the lists and answered gently: *No, no: my sweet jungefru, ye hebb me seven kysse versproke – ye mut me for den hund betale – one more – that war moi – one more, one more,* and so there was nothing for it but *one more* for quite some time until his *moy jungefrowe* seemed to get angry and said: *Wat? Schaam ge üe niet? Ick blijwe quaat – gij besmeet mij de mont – foij! üe beent van dag niet gerasseert – hoe veele soentjes sall ick dan voor en hond geeven?* Just at that moment the doorlatch creaked treacherously and she whispered: *st! st! go! ge malle portrait – go, go! my moeder kommt!* [146] – Mamma did not come but I simply could not keep myself from laughing, which is why the two of them ran off headlong, leaving behind in their haste a pink handkerchief marked G.K.

It is seldom that one gains anything from such unexpected discoveries. Actaeon surprised Diana while she was bathing and was turned into a hound for the trouble he caused. Nor was I any more successful on this occasion for, when I took the handkerchief back to my Diana and requested a kiss in exchange for my find and as a participant in their secret, I merely had my face slapped for my trouble. I am so indignant about it that I am going to shout her name for all to hear: it was that nasty – – . But no, there is no greater sin than sneaking on girls. I'll pocket the slap and hold my tongue, while exhorting every snooper who hides in doorways in order to overhear the secrets of women to take a healthy warning from the fate that befell Actaeon and myself.

I might on the other hand be hard-hearted enough to betray the red overcoat that I caught a glimpse of in the moonlight, but it is often the case that in revealing another one betrays oneself. So I shall say nothing – other than that he had presented her with a lapdog or lapbitch and that this gentlemanly dog or maidenly bitch was to be paid for with kisses – or what in Dutch coinage are called *soentjes*. I am unable to tell you the extent to which he managed to get his percentage raised later but I do know that he whispered to her behind her fan once and uttered a sigh that seemed to come all the way from his big toe as he said: *Ick onske ick kunde so well slape, as min hund, this night.*[147]

For the information of future East Indiamen I would thus like to state that anyone hoping for good luck when hunting hearts at the Cape should use lapdogs as his ammunition. All the women in the bay visited us on board one day and they ran from cabin to cabin to get hold of such items. The commandant's daughter hung on the coat-tails of our first mate in the middle of the deck and was prepared to give a promissory note to the tune of thirty *soentjes* in exchange for a little black canine treasure he had brought with him from Sweden, but neither her curtseys of supplication nor her voluptuous pink lips were capable of moving his already captive heart. We have two ship's cats on *Finland*. You can imagine how eager I was to disguise them in dogskins in order to satisfy the poor girl!

Since it bears some resemblance to the foregoing topic I should like to append a strange letter which accident delivered into my hands. It was addressed to one of the nymphs of the bay and contains all the tenderness that a seaman's bursting heart can express. The author, whose name I really don't know, seems to have heard that the women of the Cape – as well as those of the Orient in general – are much enamoured of a flowery style, and he has therefore chosen to write in that manner. I admit that I had no time to make a copy of the original but my excellent memory will make up for the lack of it. It ran something like this:

'Flower of Incomparable Beauty!
The cannon of your eyes have set light to the powder keg of my heart. My skiff has run aground on the rocks of your attractions shattering the bowsprit of my indifference so that, unless the wind of your favour soon fills the sails of my desire, I am likely to drown in the violent breakers of my desperation. Indeed, most beautiful angel, I love you more than I love a favourable wind and pieces of eight. Allow me, therefore, to drop the anchor of my desires in your Cape of Good Hope and ascertain the latitude of your Terra Incognita with the octant of my love. The compass of your eyes will hereafter determine my course and the rudder of your will steer the ship of my life. If you but knew how the fire of your beauty flamed in the oven of my heart you would surely extinguish it with the sympathetic water-pumps of your eyes. So, my coral, do not be as hard as Romans Rock, and do not crush the lantern of my burning love under the heavy iceberg of your frigidity. Please send me some loving provisions by packet-boat – or come yourself. I send you fifteen ship's barrels of greetings and remain from ballast to topgallant, in all weathers, at all points of the compass,
the Humble Keelson
of my Incomparable Mayflower,
N.N.

PS. My regards to your father and mother. I wish them a double ration of all sorts of blessings. Farewell.'

The letter was written in Dutch and the reader will probably surmise, as I did, that he was merely intending to tease his sweetheart.

Chapter XI

CONCERNING SIGONIUS AND HASENSKRÄCK[148]

On Monday the 13th of June we were all ready and bade farewell to Commandant Kirst, a man who deserves an honourable mention. His welcoming house made our stay in False Bay very pleasant, not to mention the great service he did us in the matter of victualling. Our officers had in return shown him the sort of respect that will make the Swedish flag ever welcome in this harbour.

We waited eight days for a favourable wind and our captain used this leisure time up on the hilltops, partly taking observations and partly collecting plants.

We, meanwhile, were visited by the Dutchmen from the other ship. There were among them two particularly ridiculous characters; one – a passenger to Batavia who assured us that he had translated seven of the books of Moses into Arabic, the other – a laughable *Zieketrooster* who insisted on greeting our chaplain as *myn Confrater*.[149] The former, like a dragoon in a tavern boasting of heroic deeds he has never performed, was to me the very image of Hasenskräck whereas the latter, wearing a tousled wig that was at least as old as his patched and feather-covered coat, presented an exact copy of the crazy Master Sigonius. The passenger boasted of his great wealth and beautiful slave girls. He invited every single one of our officers to honour his house in Batavia with a visit – since he knew that we would never go there – and assured them that absolutely everything, including his favourite child, would be at their service. The comforter of the sick, a master gardener at home, described the income he made from his spiritual office and, taking our pastor by the arm, assured him that he received 25 guilders monthly and 500 ditto in licence fees as well as the freedom to trade a certain quantity of schnapps, a chest of tobacco and such like, from all of which he was able to double his income when trade was going well. He then wanted to know how much the Swedish company paid out *voor de geistlichkeit op syne skipe*?[150] To which the pastor answered that he was delighted that the Dutch authorities did not muzzle the mouth of the ox that comforteth.[151] But as far as seafaring Swedish pastors were concerned, bearing in mind that their profession was very different from that of the Dutch comforter in that they did not deal either in schnapps or tobacco, they received a sufficient if meagre stipend and did not feel that they should demand more, being well aware that their kingdom was not of this world.[152] The *Ziektrooster* shrugged his shoulders and drank.

Before they left us they looked over our ship and admitted that theirs could be contained within it even though they had a crew of 350 men, half of which consisted, however, of soldiers being despatched to Batavia. At long last they bade us farewell and staggered to the rail. The passenger was still renewing his earlier offer as he climbed down the side and was still chattering about his seven books of Moses and his slave girls for a good while longer than we were capable of hearing him.

On the morning of Thursday the 21st of June we set sail, as I have already mentioned. Our passage was a quick and lucky one, which was all the more welcome to us since the cold compelled us to don our winter clothes again. Our captain did not deem it necessary on this occasion to head for the islands of St Paul and Amsterdam which ships normally make their departure point for Java; instead, we set a direct course and did not approach them any closer than two or three degrees.

Chapter XII

THE OXIAD
OR
A RESPECTFUL MEMORIAL TO OUR NORWEGIAN OX, THE WIDELY TRAVELLED ROLLO, WHO PASSED AWAY IN JUNE 1770 AND WAS INTERRED IN OUR STOMACHS THE SAME YEAR.

- – *bovis omnia plena* – Virg.[153]

It is now so long since I rhymed that you will be thinking that my vein of verse has been completely dammed. I would have thought the same had I not begun to feel it starting to drip through a couple of holes that a pair of ox horns have poked in the blockage. Let me tell you about it.

The morning after we had slaughtered our last Norwegian ox I was sent his horns as a sort of festive decoration. Each of them bore a different inscription. One of the horns, filled with boot-blacking, was to be used to ride to Blåkulla along with the witches. The other I was to keep as a symbol of the fate that awaited me in marriage.

It was this that set me contemplating the beasts of the field. All the more so since I felt that it was my duty to erect a poetic memorial over the grave of our departed Rollo in meagre recognition of the share I had received of the property of his estate. He was a fine creature and as much my travelling companion as any of the rest of them. A good many poets have scattered cypress on less worthy corpses or, to use von Dalin's expression, sung in praise of *beasts in hallowed tombs.*

– – *Boum gemitu nemus omne remugit* – [154]

Ah, Muses! Gather round my dark beshrouded lute!
Nature! Step forth in deep midwinter garb of woe!
Weep, Earth and Sea! Let not your funeral hymns be mute,
Let tears like roaring torrents down your features flow!

Ye tigers hid in Afric's jungles deep
Emerge that terror might assist me weep.
Oh, agony! – Our ox is dead.

Ye tombstone poets, so wont and quick to eulogize
Whene'er some brutish member of the human race
His race has run, help mourn my Rollo's sad demise!
'Twixt you and me the only difference I can trace
Is this: two legs not four your heroes need
And I weep gratis where you are fee'd
– But 'tis of beasts we both recite.

When you raise mighty obelisks o'er your heroes
Should mine go hence forgotten, unmourned, without song?
Never, I say! Gone are your viziers and Neroes
But their more beastly deeds remain among us long.
So come, ox world, lend me your ears,
I'll strike my lute and summon tears
To mourn your brother's fall.

His dam, a noble Jutland quadruped by birth
Whose sense of rank rejected peasant suitors' pleading,
Heard the entreaties of his sire, a bull of worth,
And bore our hero – thus a bull of breeding.
Not that a noble egg ensures a swan;
A double-barrelled name and *von*
Add nothing to the splendour of a Caesar.

Now day by day he drank at mother's gen'rous udder,
Of all the parish beasts the finest and most fair.
For warmth he wanted not, nor was there lack of fodder,
Thus loved he waxed and fattened, grew and flourished there.
Though milkmaid Lisa stole away
Several quarts from him each day
To fortify her lover.

Full grown he marched to victory upon the fields of passion
As harvester incomparable of bovine maidenheads.

His methods were the English – leave once you've had your ration!
Forget the effete compliments of bulls the French have bred!
In the course of one October
He bowled far more maidens over
Than all the Scots in Sweden in a decade.

But, alas, this brutal world brings all its heroes low
When their failing spark no longer kindles instant fire.
To a hundred beastly misses 'twas a sorrowful blow
When the knife removed the source of Rollo's pride.
Of human Rollos there are plenty
Who can please their wives at twenty
But thereafter merely slumber in the bed.

Is it so strange, then, that horns grew on his noble brow?
His many biped brothers condemned to bear the same
Could from his patient courage learn the lesson how
They too with Christian fortitude might bear the cuckold's shame.
My friend! Even when your horn grows long,
Better to hang his breeches on the prong
Than gore the one who shares your mate.

Oh, downhill, alas, downhill runs the course of Rollo's tale
For none but men of Norway could be found to pay his keep.
Exiled across the water, among beasts of foreign race,
Rollo's task – O heartless Fate! – was to plough the furrow deep.
Brutal peasants inured to toil
Expected him to till their soil
For a little straw and many vicious blows.

To see this former champion now plod with feet of clay
Enraged the gods, who whipped the sea to foam
And drove our helpless vessel from its charted way
Eastward to Norway, where the ex-bull had his home.
While we rested in the port
And enjoyed the usual naval sport
Rollo joined our crew as meaty matelot.

Though travelling steerage in the hold across wild seas
Rollo's days aboard were filled with rest and joy,
For among the sheep and goats he ruled supreme
And his welfare gave his keeper full employ.
However violent waxed the main
Rollo's stomach did remain
Replete and intact and inside.

Far south he followed us and on beyond the Cape
But now this eye that witnessed his demise must tears shed:
He's gone, alas! No more we see his once so manly shape!
Oh why, of all of us, should he alone be dead?
Well, self-interest is the fashion
And once he'd eaten up his ration
We got our own back, so to speak.

Sleep well, sweet Rollo, your fate has moved all ranks!
All that was yours in life was shared by great and small:
Your tail fell to a deckhand, midshipmen claimed your shanks,
And our scrivener has some brain where once he had none at all.
We gave your manners to the mate,
All the rest we simply ate
– But I shall keep your horns.

Those friends who thought they could put one over on me can herewith have a dose of their own medicine. I don't, however, want to involve anyone apart from those who helped to play the joke on me, for I don't have the heart to do what the Catholic princes did to the Jesuits and to tar them all with the same brush.[155]

Chapter XIII

CONCERNING THE INSTRUCTIVE HORN

Dum femina plorat, decipere laborat – [156]

On the 15th of July I saw a sea-cow. NB. On paper, that is, in a German traveller's account.

On the 16th we sighted two porpoises from the stern rail. They are fish that are distinguished by having a large horn on their heads. They were standing upright in the water and appeared to be kissing one another in something like this position.

In my simple way I asked my captain what this meant and his answer was that they were a married couple who were making love standing upright on their tails for, he added, the porpoise species behave *in coitu* just as we do. 'And you can see,' interposed our mate who was sitting alongside, 'that their marriages also resemble ours in another way. What I mean is that they have horns. The more the female kisses the male, the higher the antler sticks up above the surface of the water.' 'Yes, indeed,' sighed honest D. with his head in his hands. 'It's often been my experience that a wife is at her most loving when she has mischief in her heart.'

Good, I thought to myself. In that case I shall make a place for the porpoise in my collection of moral natural curiosities. He shall be stuffed and placed among my petrels and sharks with the following instructive inscription carved on his remarkable horn.

O!
Young.
Man. You.
Who. Go. Court-
ing. Do. Not
Choose. With. Your.
Eyes. Closed. For. The.
Waters. Of. Marriage. Are.
Perilous. One. In. Twenty.
Avoids. Shipwreck. Therefore
Take. Soundings. Keep. A. Log.
Take. Bearings. Bend. Your. Back.
In. The. Door. Where. Others. Have.
Bumped. Their. Heads. Test. The. Shallows.
Before. You. Venture. Into. The. Storm. Or.
Else. Consider. Your. Fate. In. This. Horn. That.
I. Have. Had. Erected. As. A. Warning. To. You.

What a splendid find! But how am I to keep this precious treasure? Shall I preserve it in a glass cabinet or put it in spirit? Nothing of the sort! Such methods are old-fashioned these days. I must be up-to-date. So I shall garb my porpoise in a Swedish uniform and hang a pair of tarry bellbottoms from his horn so that he is in his right element – at least, I can't think of more suitable garments for a horn-fish. For further information I shall tie a picture of a wood-sprite on the uniform, portrayed in the manner of the ancients with a wreath twined around his two horns. Under it I shall write: *Surgunt in cornua lauri*, that is, 'the wife is the husband's honour'; [157] and on the bellbottoms the reader will find the following line: *Multa tulit fecitque puer*, which translates as 'as the coat so the hanger'.[158] For while the

soldier is away fighting and the seaman is away sailing, then – –
Oh, well. *Quos ego?*[159]

The preceding event had, however, brought the conversation round to the topic of marriage. The dinner bell summoned us to table though there was no chance of food putting a stop to a topic so close to all our hearts. The conversation continued and anyone who is curious about it can follow its course in the following chapter.

Chapter XIV

AT THE SERVICE OF ALL THOSE WHO GO COURTING

'What is paradise if thou dwellest there alone,
Without the loving wife who truly makes the home?
But quick infatuation with any willing tart
Shows no more sense than hitching rides on every passing cart.'
Bishop Spegel.[160]

'When I go courting,' said one, 'I don't want merely to see the girl but, like the Turks when they are buying a horse, I want to find out about the whole breed – three or four generations back. The apple, as the proverb says, does not fall far from the tree and the sins of the fathers are usually handed down to coming generations just like certain natural disabilities. Water always tastes of the soil through which it has flowed, and when have you ever seen a healthy plant grow from tainted seed? Never! *Fortes creantur fortibus*,[161] that's what Cornelius Nepos says, isn't it, *Magister*?' – 'Yes, my dear fellow, that's what Cornelius Nepos says.' – 'Monkeys descend from monkeys, asses from asses, which is why I like to start by thumbing as carefully as possible through the family records. I would first of all investigate whether dear Grandma has got any heritable ailment. Next I would see to it that I lifted dear Grandpa's full wig to check if there were any marks on his forehead as a result of Grandma's gentleman friends. After that I would move on down to my gracious mother-in-law and check her face for any booze blemishes that might make me doubt the sobriety of the family, and finally, I should want to know how my honoured father-in-law lived in his youth. It might be that, to the detriment of his legal offspring, he either danced too much at Parisian tavern hops or spared too little of himself at London nightspots. Isn't that so, Magister?' – 'Of course, my dear fellow! He who sins will fall into the hands of the doctors.' – 'From all of this I will assess both the moral and the natural characteristics of the girl. The quality of the lineage is the best guarantee of that of the fruit and, since the upbringing of the daughter is usually left to the mother, it is reasonable to judge the daughter by her. If the mother has been a good wife I shall be able to rely on the daughter but, if the opposite holds true, I shall withdraw from the contest. *Tanti poenitere non emo,* as the philosopher said. [162] – What was his name, Magister?' – 'My dear fellow, he was ca-ca-called – sorry, I've got such a co-cough – he was called Da-Da-Darius Longimanus.'

'He could be called Longus in anus or Dr Bombastus for all I care,' continued the speaker, 'but I still like to reconnoitre the terrain before I approach the fortress. The citadel of love, just like any other citadel, has hidden mines that blow hundreds of fools to pieces. So let us make our approach with wary steps.

Once I have satisfied myself as to the quality of the kin by the methods I have mentioned, I have not the least intention of making an approach to dear father or dear mother because it is the daughter, not them, that I am courting. Her agreement should precede theirs for she is the main player in the game. It falls to the parents to advise but not to command, and I find nothing more unnatural than the oriental tyranny that gives parents the right to bring unlimited force to bear on the inclinations and marital intentions of their children. They are not the ones in danger. It is, after all, our happiness that is being decided. Should we not, then, be allowed the deciding voice in our own affairs? Are we to be driven into the bridal bed in total opposition to nature's all-powerful call as if we were yoked oxen? What demonic power! Am I not a free creature? A descendant of Adam, a man, a Christian? This hand that I eat with, this skin that

I dwell in, this heart, this foot, this – Is it not all mine? Is someone else to rule over them? Are my body, my opinions, my welfare to become mere toys to be crushed in the hands of a stranger? A prey, a – oh, it's so insufferable, Magister!' – 'Of course, my dear chap, of course; *nam quos Deus conjunxit, formyndare ne separet!*'[163] – 'Well then, I will turn to the girl first of all. Not that I intend to sing a suitor's song immediately. I still have a couple of points to be dealt with.

1. I need to know whether she has enough wit and worldly wisdom not to make me blush when we are out and despise her when we are at home, for a fool is more difficult to be saddled with than a madcap.

2. I need to be sure that our inclinations and our temperaments agree in the main. Otherwise situations could arise where she wants to cry when I have the urge to laugh, or she might be freezing under the same blanket as I am roasting.

3. Since the great slogan of marriage is 'Go forth and multiply', it seems to me that a cautious suitor should reassure himself in that respect as well. What do you think, Magister?' – 'My dear Sir, she should certainly provide a doctor's certificate! Ha, ha, ha!'

4. 'I believe that there are antipathies and sympathies between two hearts. Just as the divining-rod reveals metal and the magnet reveals the direction north, I believe that my feelings will tell me when I have met the right woman. I am not asking for romantic whimsies but it is important that I, as a person, am in the forefront of her thoughts. It's a poor portent when two lovers can look at one another without some change in the pulse rate. As for my part, I should have a poor opinion of my feelings of love if I could cross my fiancée's threshold without my blood coursing just a little, and I should likewise be put out if my arrival did not cause her just a touch of lovable embarrassment.

It is thus important to know how high we stand in the barometer of the heart before we proceed to the main question. If I discover no hindrance in any of these points I have mentioned, I shall bring up the business as a man should, with respectful freedom but not with the "ohs" and "ahs" of a simpering idiot. If she gives me a "Yes", it will then be time to move on to pappa and mamma. I shall place before them a short account of my annual income and say: "This is my property. With this and the blessing of the Lord I can provide for my wife's comfort and for the upbringing of her children. Your daughter suits me and I her. Your agreement will make us both happy."

Now, since I have already got to know the character of her parents and since I don't intend to go courting above my rank, I should be certain of their approval. There is consequently nothing left to do apart from having a word with the parson and going to bed. So, good night, gentlemen! I shall draw a curtain in front of the rest.'

Chapter XV

TO BE READ IN THE SAME BREATH AS THE FOREGOING.

'Good luck to you, Sir,' interposed another who was sitting alongside, 'but your sermon is only half done. Let's stick to the subject that the porpoise horn started us on. You have taught us how to get a good wife. Now teach us how to keep her that way.' – 'Quite so,' shouted our ship's chaplain. '*Hinc robur et securitas* as it says on the banknotes.'[164]

'Keep her that way!' our previous spokesman took up again. 'It's your own fault if she is not the same at the end as she was in the beginning. Give your wife her rightful due but, above all, rid the house of three kinds of vermin: by which I mean aged aunts, beggar women and dandies. The best of women has often been ruined by these three.

Even in the most loving marriage it might sometimes come to the stage where the husband needs to discipline his wife in one way or another. That is when the d--d old aunt steps in straightaway and starts whining about the tyranny of men. "Things were different in my youth," she says, doubling the number of wrinkles on her aged and furrowed brow. "My late husband, God bless his soul, would never have denied me anything. Whatever I pointed my finger at I got. He was so good, so good!" And here she squeezes out a tear, the toothless old crocodile, but before it has run the length of her nose, you can hear her shaking her crutch and starting off in a quite different tone of voice. "He wouldn't have dared to try that with me. True as I'm standing here before you, I'd have shown the old fellow a thing or two. I'd have put a couple of church spires on his forehead, I tell you. I wasn't ugly in those days – there were plenty of lads making eyes at me." And so she chatters on and pulls her mouth into a smile as if to draw together the few pathetic remnants of a beauty that has already withered.

What do you think about that, gentlemen? That kind of thing repeated daily can poison even the purest breast! My young wife is inexperienced, considers the things that ought to be duty as impositions, and becomes insubordinate. Her love, which had previously flowed only in my direction, looks around for other objects. The beggar women win her confidence and carry away the tittle-tattle along with their loaves of bread, and in no time at all I've got some powdered dandy hanging around ready to fish in my murky waters. If the beggar women are given the chance to gossip and the dandy the chance to inflame her excited senses with his trivial sighs and murmurs, then, alas, I can look on with horror as the mark of the porpoise sprouts on my unhappy brow. That, at least, is what the neighbours will think, which amounts to the same thing, for what pleasure do I get from having an honest wife if nobody believes it? I shall thus keep my doors permanently barred against beggar women and dandies!

But, gentlemen! I can reveal to you a method of ensuring that you have peace in your beds. An easy and natural way. Have you ever heard of a hard worker losing his job? There are no stronger bonds to bind a married couple together than swaddling. Get yourself a couple of heirs in the house as soon as possible and you will be able to defy any Asmodeus in the world.[165] A wife's interests will be centred more and more within the home. Her wandering desires will be provided with a more solid focus, will turn away from balls, theatres and parties and will centre on the dear cradle. Her husband will become daily more dear to her as she sees him reincarnated in new offspring who smilingly gurgle "mamma". The bond of loyalty, like the Gordian knot, can never be cut except by that all-conquering Alexander, DEATH. It is through the children that man and woman become one flesh. It is through the children that they grow together into one being, in the same way as two bushes on the ground push forth new shoots from their fertile stems and thus gradually plait together into one hedge. You will find, on the other hand, that the growth of horns usually occurs in infertile beds. In my study of the history of the Brotherhood of Cuckolds I, at least, have not noticed them growing except on those who have been either insufficiently industrious or insufficiently fortunate in increasing the species.

So you can see that it is our own fault if a virtuous fiancee does not remain a virtuous wife. Once you have tied her with the bonds of motherhood you can stand on your threshold with triumph on your face and say to all passing womanizers: "There is no prey for you here!" And if she is then prepared to put up with the presence of some performing cuckoo around her, you can rely on the fact that she is only doing so in order to let him say cuckoo to your children. That's what I think.'

Chapter XVI.

A SLICE OF THE SAME PIE.

'First class thinking, especially on those final points,' answered another speaker who hadn't yet voiced an opinion. 'But your scruples regarding your wife's ancestry seem to me to be more than somewhat superfluous. While you are still hanging around the peripheries, someone bolder might run off with the fortress. A hundred pretty women could be snatched away in less than the time you have been talking about it. No, I prefer to take them by surprise. I shall catch my wife before any mortal soul has even had time to think of her. Listen to what I intend to do!

I never waste a glance on girls who have reached what is regarded as a marriageable age because they are already ruined to a great extent by novels, aged aunts and the idle chatter of dandies. Evil has already taken root in them and wilfulness, domineering ways, pleasure-seeking and a hundred other fancies have already had time to become fixed. They are like a brittle old branch which can no longer be bent without the risk of breaking it. The husband is compelled either to abdicate all his rights as a husband or else to defend himself with his fists. I find neither thought pleasing since my ambition is to be both loved like a husband and feared like a father.

For that reason I intend to hook myself a girl still in sewing school. She will be fourteen years old, and absolutely definitely not over sixteen. I shall then be in a position to mould her according to my own inclinations. A young branch obeys the hand of the gardener. It will be possible to accustom her to her housewifely duties by persuasion and by the maturity of my common sense without recourse to trouble and force. To make the whole business that much easier I shall preferably turn my attentions on a maiden for whom my offer will come as a benefaction and thus gratitude no less than love will bind her heart to me. I am assuming, of course, that I shall not marry until I can do so without having to take a dowry into account. It will be quite another matter if I am poor. In the first mentioned case, however, I shall have the joy of observing my growing flower daily developing pleasing new qualities in my arms whereas a mature girl would already be tending to fade in the same situation; I should also find in her a tender wife whose most indulgent caresses are mixed with innocence and a lovable touch of timorousness. I shall in good time have centred all her likes, inclinations and pleasures upon myself so that they cannot turn in any other direction. Even before she has had time to look around in the realm of seduction, she will be saved – and with her, my forehead.

In other respects I agree with your plans, Sir, and would merely like to add one small but important observation. I don't know how many times I have been angered by the sight of a crowd of unwashed and undressed women going carelessly about the house all day long! "I have no interest in pleasing anyone but my husband," is what they say – as though he were a lover of filth. Fie! As a compliment it is far too smelly, and every time I heard a remark of that sort cross my wife's lips I should look sulky for a week. Since I myself like to be properly dressed, I insist that she too should go straight from bed to her toilet, otherwise she could very quickly become a very everyday face to me and – '

'No! Wait now, gentlemen!' someone else shouted, throwing away his spoon. 'I simply can't put up with listening to you any longer. What in the name of a barrel of monkeys do you want? Were my lady to show any desire to rebel I should soon let the birch dust the lust out of her sinful hide so that her ribs ached. I may have taken her for my own advantage but certainly not to have her sitting in front of her mirror pulling faces at canon law. I have taken her to bake bread out of my flour, not for her to use it as hair powder. If she is not capable of weaving her own clothes then the lazy bitch can tie a leafy twig over her nether parts like her mother Eve! Am I supposed to work my fingers to the bone for a parrot who has her nose stuck in a bottle of smelling salts all day, who sits around with a comb in her fist instead of a distaff, and who is afflicted by polite vapours, Froggy swoons and God knows what else? No thank you, my pretty boys, I'm not having my house turned into a hairdresser's shop! I fail to understand this new-fangled effeminate age you live in. Your are afraid of getting horns like porpoises and yet you are putting them there yourselves thanks to the excessive compliance with which you support your womenfolk in lust and vanity, thus providing them an easy path to all kinds of lechery and devilment! You never heard much about cuckolds in the old days when a housewife wasn't ashamed to go into the kitchen or the brew house, but nowadays the devil and the Frenchy rule. Our soldiers have turned into rabbits and our women into wh-res. Modesty waved good-bye to the latter at the same time as bravery to the former. Both of them have now learned to dance like that damned French cockerel. *O tempora, o mores*![166] – Do you want to know what sort of welcome I give to dandies? I live close to the highway and it happens from time to time that some officer on the make or some impertinent little secretary gets wind of my harem. They immediately smother me with a million polite excuses for having taken the liberty of inconveniencing me with their visits but claim to have been unable to withstand the pleasure of seeing how I live and learning on the spot from my well-being. They are so inordinately pleased that my wife is well and they trust that the precious health of the *mamselles* still continues. – I bow and assure them sincerely that all are well and, as to their interest in how I live, I am ready at once to take the measure of their friendly curiosity. – At which I drag the gentlemen all round my estates until the lust begins to drip from their brows, and then while we are viewing my barn I ask humbly whether it would amuse them to test their skill with a flail. – In a flash they have shouted to the groom to saddle their horses and before I have time to tell them that they will be welcome to come again they have set spurs to the horse and galloped out of sight. Not a single one of them has yet done my house the honour of remaining overnight. I then tell my wife about the prank and we both laugh heartily. – Take the first girl you like as your fiancée, give her plenty to keep her busy and then she won't kick over the traces. If that doesn't help, then – Watch out! It's out with the birch! "Balaam's ass became eloquent when she was driven with a whip", as von Dalin says.'[167]

We all admitted that this cure was the most effective one even if more than a little Russian. In spite of that, most people considered it reasonable in extreme cases, particularly our chaplian, who supported it with the examples of Gustav I and Karl XI.

'But,' continued the former speaker, 'I do not wish to suggest that everyone is justified in beating an unfaithful wife, for a goodly number of men deserve their horns. I would therefore not allow the following to do so:

1. Worn-out old men who have taken young girls unto themselves should not use the birch for it is not with the arm that they should be proving their manhood.

2. May the same rule apply to those who have entered into marriage from common self-interest or without the full consent of the maiden. The former would appear to merit the stigma and the latter to have acquiesced thereto.

3. To be included in the same category are those exhausted bachelors who have smuggled the worthless remains of their lecherous youth into the bosom of a healthy maiden, for such men deserve to suffer what their misdeeds have made them liable to.'

'So be it!' exclaimed our chaplain, taking his glass from his lips. 'As to the last two points, I sing Amen from the bottom of my heart, for "t'is better that the Ground should be ploughed by asses than lie quite untill'd", as Bishop Burnet said on the day that he inducted a dozen bad curates.[168] But in what manner have the unfortunate old men transgressed? They have to have someone to keep them warm, after all! No one looked askance at David when he took a maiden unto himself to warm his feet in his old age.[169] If the old fellow can substitute other comforts for what he lacks in the one particular, it is a pity to grudge him his little bedwarmer.'

'Well, we could always exempt parsons instead, then, since they pay court to the benefice rather than the widow,' the others answered, laughing so much that it set up waves in the punch-bowl.

'O Belial, Belial, there is death in the pot!'[170] the chaaplain shouted with a face as long as the longer catechism. 'No, gentlemen, if parsons deserve any sort of crown on their heads, it is a martyr's crown, for they sacrifice everything – even their own bodies – for the sake of an act of mercy. But since we have to decide who should fill that vacant slot we could fill it with married seamen who go with a tart in Cadiz or with a Hottentot at the Cape. A glass of punch, Bredberg!'

Chapter XVII

FAR SMALLER THAN THE PUNCH-BOWL IT DEALS WITH

'Bring on the dessert, steward!' shouted our captain and leader, putting an end to all our thoughts of marriage.

Dessert? At sea? I hear you ask. – Yes, indeed. Oranges, pineapples, raisins, grapefruit and anything else that you can't get at home we can get here. The very thing that you might think we have in abundance – that is, fish – is precisely what we lack most and it is seldom served. In this respect you can apply the proverb about the blacksmith's mare and the shoemaker's wife to us: they, it is said, are always the worst shod just as we have the least access to fish even though we are in the middle of the fishy realm.

We dine excellently aboard ship and anyone who denies it deserves to die of hunger or, what comes to the same thing, to be tossed aboard a barge with a miser in command. You won't need to pick your teeth after brisket and veal cutlets there. My son has been on that galley. I learned that lesson during my long voyage home from London in 1769. Stock-fish and peas at noon, peas and stock-fish in the evening. Ditto yesterday, ditto today and ditto for three endless weeks so that my whole person came close to being turned into a pot of peas. I shall never forget how I paced the deck in throes of agony sighing 'O Lord preserve us from misers, contrary winds and ship's food etc.' But now I am singing a quite different tune. On our departure from the Cape we were carrying five or six hundred living and edible creatures with us, not to mention several cartloads of fruit and fine wines. May God bless those who put up the money! Menu, service and abundance – they all redound to the honour of those who equipped us.

As to our crews, they are on the whole far better catered for than those of other nations. Apart from three solid meals a day the company provides them with tea twice a day and schnapps once, or more often when the work is hard – for instance, in stormy weather, on making a landfall or when raising the anchor. The signal for schnapps is the clanging of a bell: music that the sailors wouldn't swop for the best concerts in Stockholm.

They also get punch twice a week. At one o'clock on Wednesdays and Sundays the chief steward comes marching along from the bows with a copper ladle on his shoulder. Behind him walk two strong-armed sailors bearing between them an iron-shod tub big enough to drown the fattest dragoon in. This is carried up onto the half-deck where its liquid contents are glorified in a short discourse on drink. The people are called together by the usual ringing melody and they gather like flies round a bowl of sour milk, waiting with thirsty throats for the refreshing words of the sermon. The chief steward stands up and begins his evensong. The opening words are: "Come hither and drink!" This is a text that he expounds in 130 parts, and in the process of doing so he attracts more listeners than any priest has yet had at high mass. Which is hardly surprising since the latter shouts the opposite: "Be on your guard against gluttony and drunkenness!" Very different texts and consequently they have very different results. The former sets their legs up ready for a jolly reel, the latter gives them long faces and lulls them into a devout slumber. What more proof is needed that a seaman has more feeling in his throat than in his heart? – Everyone holds out a container. Some of them have old wooden mugs, some hollowed-out coconuts, some simply the crowns of their hats. It is a pleasure to see their expressions growing brighter and brighter. They receive enough to get happy but too little to get rowdy. So the result of such banquets is no worse than a couple of friendly toasts or a boisterous reel around the deck.

Were I in my moralizing mood I would suggest that all parties held ashore were organized in like manner, for it is deplorable that a host measures his honour by the greater or lesser intoxication of his guests.

Chapter XVIII

ARRIVAL IN JAVA

On the 3rd of August, six weeks after our departure from the Cape of Good Hope, we sighted the island of Java and after sailing along the coast for three days we rounded its extreme tip – what they call Java Head – and arrived on the 8th ditto in Anjer, which is where the ships of the East India Co. usually anchor to take on water and refreshment. A Dutch corporal had, meanwhile, brought a couple of turtles aboard, along with the news that *Prins Gustav* had already passed this way nine weeks ahead of us. This was all the more surprising to us since we knew that she had lain in Cadiz for twenty days and we ourselves had made a speedy passage from Norway, but on reflection we realized that she had not even had a suspicion of the hurricane that had chased us into Svinörsund, and that was the explanation. Which, however, did not stop our cook from clapping his sooty hands and saying: 'If you've got the devil as an uncle you'll soon reach Ch-China.'

It would be impossible to find anywhere on the globe with more beautiful views than those presented to the passing sailor by the coast of Java on one side and that of Sumatra on the other. The endlessly green shoreline, shaded by straight and majestic trees that either rise gradually from large rounded hills or spread as hedges and green labyrinths in all the smoother valleys, creates a paradise garden utterly beautiful to the eye at the same time as it delights the nose with its sweet, refreshing fragrance. There is not a sandy hill, not a bare cliff, not a scraggy jumble of stones to spoil it. How splendid Paradise must have been if the Lord of nature has built such a beautiful dwelling place even for the monkeys!

In the evening, when we were in the region of Java Head, we encountered a booby-bird sailing along on a branch. I was pleased to observe how securely he was sitting aboard his little leafy vessel and he appeared to be holding a course for the other shore. I recalled the poets of old who maintained that man had learned from the swine how to plough the earth, and it occurred to me that it might similarly have been a booby that gave us the first inkling of seamanship. This supposition led me further. I guessed that the nightingale must have been our teacher of music, the fox of political wisdom, the ant of economics and the tiger of military theory, for in this last field I don't want to be as harsh as Milton, who assures us in his *Paradise Lost* that all military weaponry, especially muskets, mortars and cannon, were forged in the abyss and loaded by devils.[171] My guess seems to me to have a far better foundation, and I have found on closer examination that those who pursue these arts, each in his own field, still possess the nature, habits and principles of their respective originators. Had I not forcibly reined in my galloping imagination, I should have gone still farther. I was on the point of christening councillors as pupils of the ox, quacks as deacons of the raven, dandies as apprentices of the ape, excisemen as journeymen of the dog and so on to the point where I could well have found myself involved in a war with the most dangerous wasps of the punchbowl this side of the moon. But I shall hold my tongue and see instead how my original thoughts run as verse:

Mother Nature's
Other creatures
Provide the inspiration.
Our sailor men
Took all they ken
From booby navigation.

We learned to plough
From friendly sow
Not farmers' innovation.
Heroic wars
Are fought with claws
At tigers' instigation.

Our feathered kin
Who sweetly sing
Imparted composition,
While foxy skills
Can cure the ills
That fester 'tween the nations.

'Twas Maître Daw
Who taught that law
Is merely litigation.
So now you know
Why high and low
Resemble brute creation.

Chapter XIX

SUMMARY REPORT

- – *Acheronta movebo* – Virg.[172]

In this the third Finnish expedition I do not recall any dishonest statement that needs to be apologised for, though I can be called to account for other trifling matters.

In my opinions of the Cape my pen seems to have followed an uneven course and it is possible that I contradict myself in a number of places where I have a mixture of paeans and satire. But where is the perfection that cannot tolerate some shadow? Moral matters do, after all, have hundreds of aspects so how can they be painted in monochrome?

People might, of course, whisper that I slander seaman unfairly, but anyone who claims that is repaying an imagined injustice with a real one. Quite the reverse is true: I have all the respect for this useful class of citizens of the realm that any patriot could demand, and I sincerely wish that we had as many again of them as we already have so that the economy of the country in general could blossom and expand along with their personal economies.

But tell me of a flock that does not have its scabby sheep. Even holy orders are not without them. Is it any wonder, then, that an estate as worldly as that of seamen should offer the occasional subject for satire?

They themselves could hardly deny that a host of foolish, if bold, maritime peasants are to be found among their number. What else can you call people who on the one hand look with scorn on everything to do with knowledge and on the other hand make a virtue out of rough and wild behaviour as though ignorance and vulgarity were essential features of a bold sailor?

No one demands that a seaman should be learned, even less that he should be a courtier, but since navigation is not a handicraft but actually an important province in the realm of science, and since a captain can be said to represent not just his crew but also to some extent his nation in all the foreign places he comes to, it is reasonable to expect that anyone who ever achieves command of a ship should be in possession of both a clear head and civilized manners. No one is accepted as an officer in the Dutch service until he has undergone an examination in various fields of knowledge and I am witness to the fact that a Swede, who had been a first mate at home and now wanted to sail out of Amsterdam, had to make considerable improvements to his geometry and mathematics in spite of his good qualifications before he could get a less important post than the one he had occupied in his native country. As far as customs are concerned, I certainly don't hold up the Dutch as an example for they are the most barbaric and uncivilized of all seafaring rabble, probably as a result of the motley mob scraped together by white slavers and press gangs and thrown aboard their ships. But since communal existence, particularly within the narrow confines of the ship's rails where the same old faces are seen all the time and thus very likely to become tiresome, is intolerable without mutual tolerance and humanity, it seems to me that good social habits can never be emphasized too much. I admit that the commander aboard a ship very often needs strict discipline and a thundering bass voice to keep his bold sailors in check but he should not need to extend this to the higher ranks, far less should it follow him ashore. The boatswain's manner must be laid aside along with his tarry trousers.

There are situations in which a seaman who has been hatched and fledged on salt water, so to speak, sometimes does not have the opportunity either to reinforce his experience with learning or to civilize his person with a knowledge of proper social behaviour. I have no desire to attack such a man as long as he goes about his business without scorning those who are acquainted with knowledge and without pestering his fellow men with filthy vulgarities. But when he refers to the first-mentioned as swots and the second as blackguards, no one will object to me hanging the sign of the ox on his brow as a righteous warning to his fellows; he is, after all, displaying at one and the same time vulgar ingratitude and manifestly stupid crudity. Who was it who described for him the course of the stars, put the compass in his hand, measured the globe that he sails upon or gave him the octant with which he navigates across the deep if it was not these swots that he laughs at so unashamedly? Do not their sleepless nights, their ruined health, their mental toils and struggles make them worthy of some other reward? Judge for yourselves whether the Englishman is lying when he calls men like that *sea-brutes*! What, moreover, can be a greater disgrace to mankind than a naval officer who not only has the right to command his subordinates but has also taken to imitating them by living like a filthy Muscovite and who, by his dirty bosun's manners and harsh vulgarities, makes life foul for those who have the misfortune to live with him aboard. When such a man comes into the company of foreigners he is a stain on the reputation of the whole of his nation, not to mention the fact that any decent lad who happens to be under his command will be mocked and detested simply because he insists on being civilized and refuses to degrade his sensible nature to the same animal style of life as his superior.

I shall wage war on all such peasants of the sea as long as there is a drop of ink flowing in my ink-well, though there is no one more willing than me to give honour where honour is due. A seaman who brings together the necessary insights into his own trade with polite habits and at least some respect for genius is rightly considered to be among the most useful and consequently valuable constituents of the realm. Which is why I shall always be found as ready and willing to praise the latter type as to criticize the former.

No one should imagine that I have gathered the foregoing critical observations within the rails of *Finland*. I have already pointed out that my captain's name is Ekeberg, a name which by itself should be sufficient to refute any such suspicion; and it is, moreover, a pleasure for me to acknowledge that I have met none but men of good character among the rest of my travelling companions. But this is not the first time that I have been aboard ship. I have seen and associated with seafarers, both our own and those from abroad, long before this voyage. These present thoughts are, thus, no more than general conclusions reached from the experience of earlier years and anyone who imagines that I am concealing some personal bitterness in them is doing a great injustice both to truth and to my heart. The occasional dart that I have fired should not be allowed to provide the justification for such a unkind interpretation.

Finally, I am well aware of the fact that a great deal of what I have noted in this book is likely to be both incomprehensible and tedious to those who have never been in such a situation. That can't be helped. It has given me considerable pleasure to spend my leisure hours in this way and those friends who read what I have written should perhaps take a careful look at how they pass theirs.

I shall be happy if they want to accompany me further. Whether they do or don't, let us finish *my third Finnish expedition* here.

Here I stand
On the sand
Out in Java:
What I learn
And discern
You shall gather.

Next I'll go
Floating slow
Up to Canton,
And like here
I shall sneer
At what I chance on.

If you care
And can bear
Still to read me,
Read some more -
If not, snore
And don't heed me.

The Fourth Finnish Expedition
From Java to China

Chapter I

Defessi Aeneadae quae proxima cursu
Contendunt petere – - Virg.[173]

The anchor had no sooner hit the bottom than alongside came two Javanese proas laden with hens, monkeys, turtles, parrots and all kinds of fruit, coconuts, bananas etc. They carry on a particularly flourishing trade in rattan here. The seamen bartered for these goods with old shirts, mirrors and razors. Firearms and powder were what the Javanese most desired, though the Dutch had forbidden them to trade in these items. There was a soldier from Anjer present to keep a watchful eye out but in spite of that scores of rusty muskets and pistols were smuggled over the side. He was from Saxony and seemed to be following the sensible rule of live and let live. Our captain forbade us to trade in monkeys for the simple reason that we already had enough of that sort back at home.

The launch was going ashore so I and a few other friends were given an opportunity to visit Anjer. All along the shore we were met by a little fleet of small punts, hollowed out like long drinking or kneading troughs. There was a naked boy sitting in each of them and the short paddle he used was flattened like a spade at both ends; they tossed these from one side of their punts to the other at an amazing speed and seemed to be racing against the fish. Even including their loads these vessels were no larger than could quite comfortably be swallowed whole by an ordinary sized crocodile. The lads looked at us and laughed as if to say: 'You poor blighters, you can't get up any sort of speed with less than nine oars.' That is the number our launch had.

Exceptionally pleasant as this country may look, it is very uncomfortable on account of the suffocating heat accompanied by torrential showers of rain and ever-present thunder and lightning. It is a not uncommon occurrence for ships to be struck by lightning. It had happened to our ship on its previous voyage and it is very common in the Batavia Roads. Until you get used to it, it is quite frightening to listen to the long, drawn-out claps rolling between the clouds overhead and hurling hissing flames that threaten to set the whole vault of heaven alight.

We took a trip into the forest. It was fun to watch the monkeys leaping about in one tree while talkative parrots sat in the next tree seemingly laughing at their hilarious capers. But the pleasures of wandering around are dearly bought when you are forced to keep your eyes skinned and muskets ready for tigers and crocodiles lurking on the right hand side or a swarm of poisonous green snakes hanging from the branches on the left. The actual danger is not perhaps that great but simply imagining it is quite enough in itself. I was told that a tiger had bitten the head off a Prussian first mate here and his bloodstained ghost seemed to reveal itself in every bush as a warning.

I shall say about Java what an Englishman said about Paoli when he came to London in 1769: 'Respect grows with distance.'[174] I should have taken this land to be a paradise if I had never set foot here, but now it seems to me like a beautiful girl who has been conquered after a long struggle: in hope she was a goddess, in possession just an everyday girl. The objects of our desires shine brightly from afar; close up they are nothing. One embraces the shadow instead of the reality, is brought down to earth and calls out: 'O vanity of vanities!'[175] Oxenstierna likens an honest friend to the Phoenix: it is something everyone talks about and no one possesses.[176] Why did he not say the same thing about happiness?

Anjer is a small Javanese town, if a collection of hastily-erected bamboo huts full of two-legged monkeys can be called that. The Dutch, who are sole rulers of the country having gradually driven out the Danes and the English, keep a strong garrison here. It consists of a corporal and five common soldiers who are posted one to each native village along the coast. Their arsenal is on the same scale: it comprises two good blunderbusses with flintlocks and four without, and six sabres with brass hilts. That is all that is necessary to hold several thousand Javanese in check. That's how worthless people are when they lack both knowledge and sound habits.

The religion of the country's native inhabitants is Mohammedan, both here and in the greater part of the neighbouring larger islands of Borneo, Sumatra and the rest. This plague has thus spread not only to the outer fringes of the continents but has even crossed the sea. How it has been able to spread so far from the prophet's homeland is an important question. Did he have missionaries as the Pope does and, if he did, how did they cross the sea? Has anyone ever heard of a Muslim flag in these waters?

It was Friday evening. The corporal, a Swede called Gestrin, showed me a Muslim religious service. As far as externals are concerned it was similar to that of the Jews. They sat by the light of a number of weak lamps, rocked their heads and mumbled between their teeth a whole host of things that Mohammed and I probably understood about equally. Their church was built of stone and was a square low building with grills instead of windows. It looks just like the Russian prison building between the Kronan redoubt and Gothenburg but is covered with pantiles from Holland. The women as well as the men are present. Their mufti or priest, if I can call him that, along with his wife were separated from the others by a piece of white cloth that they had thrown over themselves.

Towards nightfall they light numerous fires along the shore and I was told that this was to frighten away wild animals.

Chapter II

CONTINUATION

Optat ephippia bos - - Horat. [177]

The Javanese who had illegally managed to acquire old firearms aboard ship ran off into the forest to test-fire them. The younger of them started off by firing priming charges but gradually became accustomed to stronger detonations; the older men shot more boldly but their aim was bad. We could hear the cracking of their guns far into the night.

I asked the corporal how the Dutch dared allow this to go on since their safety depended on the ignorance of the Javanese in such matters, and he answered that it had initially been strictly forbidden but lately became permissible as a means of exterminating the wild animals. And when I then suggested that they might start with tigers and finish with the Dutch, he was of the opinion that there was no danger unless they gained access to heavier artillery. He did, however, describe them as an unreliable race and assured me that he and his colleague never dared to sleep both at the same time.

I then asked him why he had left Sweden, to which he shrugged and said that there was no freedom there. Here, on the other hand, he was permitted to draw his monthly wage and to carry on a little trading on the side, as well as keep mistresses etc. I thus found in him the same thing as is to be found in all deserters from Sweden: they confuse the concepts of freedom and licence. Their home country is made to take the blame for what is actually a result of their own sloth and profligacy. They boast of their well-being in foreign parts whereas their swollen jaws bear witness to hunger and misery. There are hundreds of them running around London and Amsterdam praising their foreign freedom, which in actual fact consists of nothing but the chance, as patrons of some licentious whorehouse on Sundays, to dispose of everything they have earned in the week. It is only fanatics of gewgaws and frippery who are unhappy at home in Sweden, and that is as it should be, since we ought to prefer that which is useful to that which is merely nice to have. I refuted Sir Corporal's case as well as I was able, demonstrating to him that if freedom in the true sense does not exist in Sweden then it does not exist anywhere.

'Yes, but that doesn't put food in your belly,' he interposed. I suggested that he take a look at our pot-bellied clerics, fleshy squires and well-nourished farmers. Put these on one side of a set of scales along with Stockholm brewers, bakers and butchers and fill the other side with Dutch cheesemongers, baggy-trousered skippers, beer-gutted tavern-keepers, rolls of tobacco, pipes and the like, as well as deacons and madams, and you will find that your side is still utterly outweighed. The Swedes are not so light as their currency. Genius can get by comfortably enough and industriousness can feed itself well but indolence starves. If there are occasions when money and privilege ride roughshod over merit, you can comfort yourself with the thought that the same thing happens everywhere.

'That may be so,' he continued, 'but I know that in my line of business with the musket and drum no-one gets far unless his name has a d – d *von* in front of it or a bl – y *hielm* tagged on the end.' At this point he walked back and forth three times so vigorously that the bamboo beams creaked under him. I thought he was trying to demonstrate light infantry pace so I kept quiet. And, anyway, I could not contradict him on this point.

He calmed down and we lighted our pipes. At that very moment a ghostly apparition, so ugly that I dropped my pipe in terror and almost fell off the chair, came through the door bearing a white child at her breast. I was about to ask him in a trembling voice whether it was the custom in this country to employ wet-nurses from the underworld when he forestalled me by assuring me that this was his *concubina*. I broke out in a cold sweat and I cannot remember whether I congratulated him or not, but I can still remember her witch-like appearance so vividly that I could sketch it line by line in all its nastiness if I were not afraid of causing pregnant women to abort in terror. The task would be made that much easier by the fact that she appeared in her negligé and was otherwise only dressed in a piece of blue cloth around her waist, thus all of her voluminous attractions were fully revealed to my eyes.

Had she been as black as a Moor or an even yellowish-brown like a Hottentot I would have called her bearable, but there were green diamond-shaped marks, yellow crescents and streaky black clubs scattered at random on her ashen skin. It looked to me as if all the Cupids on the island had come together to paint her but had been unable to agree on the primary colours and had started arguing just like the builders of Babel; in the confusion they had spilt red lead, white lead, umber and gutta-percha together and then taken to their heels. Projecting of jaw and grinning like a monkey she showed me two rows of teeth the colour of blood and with long strands of the betel she was chewing sticking out of them. Her eyes were dark-brown, bleary and dripping, and they appeared to be edged with red frieze. When she walked I could count all the muscles and veins in her shrunken calves since they twisted and turned between her flesh and her skin in numerous blue meanderings as if representing a map full of rivers, streams and brooks. When I add to this that her breasts, or udders to be more accurate, hung down round her waist like two pendulous bagpipes, you will all understand that our corporal had every reason to decamp from an oppressive Sweden for the sake of such a sweetheart. He had two children by her, he said, and assured me that she had been far more beautiful in the past than she was now. She loved him to the point of madness and would drown herself if she ever noticed that he was intending to desert her etc. I asked him whether his children were baptised, assuring him that if such were not the case our chaplain would be pleased to bring them into the Christian faith. He answered no, but added that there was no great hurry about it. They were thus like their mother in the matter of religion even though in all other respects they were the very image of their father: white and well-favoured.

Chapter III

MORE ABOUT THE CORPORAL

Foenum habet in cornu, longe fuge – Horat. [178]

The corporal was pleasant enough but how can a Swede forgive him his attitude to his homeland? When asked why he did not visit us aboard ship he answered abruptly: 'What's there for me in that? There's nothing to be gained by it.' I found this an indescribably tedious answer because I don't feel that we should have given him anything, unless it was an old plumb-line to hang himself with. I can't be doing with all these absconded Swedes I meet abroad and they seem to me like so many criminals. And what am I to conclude anyway about their moral characters since they have shown themselves capable of forgetting that noblest of all a citizen's duties – love for his homeland? If I were to desert the motherland that gave me life, education and Christianity and to trample scornfully upon the grave-mounds of my fathers, would it not reveal an ingratitude worthy of the gallows? So what are we to say about people of that sort when they cling to the coat-tails of a visiting countryman in order to beg a service, a gift or a meal? A Turk is more deserving of my sympathy. Those who are unfortunate should be helped everywhere but the renegade can starve even if he is my brother.

Meanwhile, however, we were blasting smoke at one another from a couple of long Dutch pipes. He described the country to me and did his best to fill me with a mixture of lies and truth about, for instance, the magic arts of the Javanese, snake-charming, tiger sorcery and the old men of the forest. But since I had already gone through a number of travellers' descriptions of Java I was more often than not able to point out his mistakes. In the following matters I have some confidence in his account.

The Dutch militia, he told me, numbers 12 000 men on the whole island, half of them being Europeans. This number could be doubled in an emergency. In the interior of the country, however, there were still unsubjugated kings but all around the coasts the Dutch had fortresses and settlements. The governing body, *Raath van Indien* [179] to which all the other Dutch possessions in this part of the world are also subject, had its seat in Batavia where there was a garrison of 5000 men. Bantam, which used to be the capital of the island though it has now suffered considerable devastation, was situated a dozen or so miles from Anjer and had its own king; he had initially been given a good deal of respect and had an ambassador in London but now he is nothing but a Dutch subject. The corporal had seen his court and the harem consisted of several hundred concubines, they catering for all of the king's wants since men were never allowed entry to the inner court. A year ago his favourite sultana was said to have given birth to twins, one of them white and the other dark-brown, and all the wise men and doctors in Java were summoned to explain how this had happened. The matter remained undecided but the Dutch soldiers – there is a garrison of two or three hundred of them there – solved the riddle for themselves and laughed. It is forbidden on pain of death to molest the women but since His Bantamese Majesty cannot stretch to all his nymphs at once, and since the latter harbour a considerable respect for the manhood of Europeans, it happens from time to time that a doughty warrior slips stealthily in over the wall and makes a successful surprise attack.

The attempt does, however, sometimes end on the gallows for I was told that one soldier was caught and hanged. My corporal called this 'dying on the bed of honour' since the soldier had died in an assault. – I would not have believed this story had I not been assured of its veracity by another officer, whose post was right opposite us on the coast of Sumatra and who recounted the affair in question in the same words. It is not in itself incomprehensible since several of my travelling companions who had been delayed in Poulo-Condore three or four years back told me that they had lived like members of the family with the island's princesses as long as they had a bottle of perfume or some other nice trinket to offer them.

When one reads of the overthrow of Indian states and sees that all over both Asia and Africa there are great and populous races enslaved in European chains – partly subjugated by the bloody use of weapons and partly by a barbaric slave-trade – then Noah's prophecy concerning his three sons and their descendants is revealed with absolute clarity: 'God shall enlarge Japheth, and he shall dwell in the tents of Shem; and Canaan shall be his servant.'[180] This has been fulfilled to a tee, as long as we assume that the first-named pitched his tents in Europe while the other two occupied Asia and Africa. Europeans fill me with wonder when I see them overthrow mighty thrones with no more than a handful of men, but when, on the other hand, I consider the bloody barbarities which have sullied their conquests, I am almost led into thinking along with Rousseau that civilization and learning can make a race more powerful without making it in any way better. It makes my hair stand on end when I read of a band of dirty sailors breaking into the palaces of princes, trampling crowned heads underfoot and hanging their tarry trousers up on royal spires. There was an unfortunate king of Madura who was chased from his ancestral kingdom in his old age and flees in a small boat with all that is dear to him – his wives and children – to his brother-in-law, the ruling prince of Borneo. A skipper from Batavia is sent in pursuit of him and this so frightens his brother-in-law that he refuses to receive him. An English East Indiaman is anchored in the roadstead. The king buys himself protection on board this ship with a mass of jewels and precious stones which he takes from the ears of his womenfolk. The Dutch skipper schemes and threatens. What happens? The unfortunate monarch and the whole of his weeping family are handed over, clapped in irons and dragged back to be punished as rebels because he had dared to defend his subjects' freedom and lives against a passing swarm of men of violence drawn hither from Europe by greed. This happened here in 17.. .[181]

What do you think? Has our enlightened age improved the human heart? I don't know who bears the greater shame: the Dutchman who received him or the Englishman who handed him over.

Chapter IV

FROM WHICH THERE SHOULD EMERGE ONE OR TWO WORDS ABOUT LOVE.

Quisquis amat ranam, ranam putat esse Dianam. [182]

The natural inhabitants of the island are for the most part small in stature but well-fleshed and merry. They are of a blackish-brown colour. The womenfolk, or as many of them as I saw, seemed to be designed solely with suitors from Blåkulla in mind and they resemble in every particular the corporal's wife I have already described. Their mouths are wide and protruding, hair and eyes are raven black, noses flat and teeth syrup-red from the betel root they chew continuously. They oil their skin with coconut oil so that it is all shiny. For my taste their appearance is a powerful antidote to love.

They can, however, be little goddesses to the eyes of a Javanese youth, and one of our Swedish beauties would probably have as little luck here as one of theirs would have in Sweden. We paint our devils black; those of the Africans are white. Taste can take many forms. Habit can make anything tolerable, even the corporal and his sweet sultana, for instance.

Were a sighing suitor in Java to go off into the moonlight to complain of his cruel shepherdess I imagine that he would roll in the dirt, invoke nature and give sniffling expression to his despairing love in something like the following wise:

Still, booby, still, in solitude I weep!
Hold, parrot, hold, thy voice is but forlorn
Since Tirsa now thy company dost scorn.
Thou lantern of the night that shimrest o'er the deep,
How canst thou shine when Tirsa hides away?
Cloak thy light in cloud if thou wouldst soothe my pain.
Such sounds I hear! Let trees here silent be
And winds fall still, ashamed to blow
Where tears for Tirsa down my cheeks do flow.
Together here we oft did guard her sheep,

Here sat my love as pretty as the morn
And spoke of loyal hearts in love's sweet dawn.
Her wondrous skin, on which the oily sheen
Of coconut did mirror the tropic sun,
Entranced my eye and soon my heart had won.
Her pretty mouth, with betel juice agleam,
Had not its equal 'mongst all of Java's maids:
Each tooth stood forth with cinnob redness stained.
Her fleshy lips, as curved as bows can be,
Were brown in hue below the lumpy nose
That captivated shepherds by the drove.
But what were these against that divine stream
Of light that shot from dark yet fiery eyes
As lightning illuminates nocturnal skies?
The gods of heaven with all the power they wield
Own not a thunderbolt of equal might
To set the heart within my breast alight.

How empty now the meadow and the field
Where once my shepherdess did sweetly sport
Revealing all the beauties that I sought.
Her pretty breasts she rested on her knees,
Heavy as the grapes in some enormous bunch,
And when I crept to taste again my childhood lunch
She'd throw them with a look of girlish tease
Over her shoulder and then laugh with joy
To see my disappointment at her ploy.
I well recall how, body full of sleep,
I laid me in the meadow grass to rest
And she, all tenderness, enfolded me in breast.
She brought refreshing nectar from the stream
And from her lips she fed me divine food
Along with betel nut already chewed.
O happy time! Why didst thou ever flee?
For Tirsa, too, has followed in your train
And left me weeping here a lovelorn swain.

Perchance she's false, perchance she sits upon another's knee!
Arise, ye oceans, swallow up my life,
I will not live if she's another's wife!
Oh, she is cruel! Three times from out the sea
The seeing moon has ris' and thrice gone down
Since Tirsa made her loving presence known.
Three times has darkness cloaked the earthly scene,
Three times the folk of earth have sweetly slept
While my tired eyes of slumber are bereft.
Three nights the dew has dilute been with tears,
Three nights the wind hath borne my sorrowing wail,
Oh, Tirsa, say not our love shall not prevail!
Thou knowest not the hearts that thou hast speared!
Vandal! Well then, since it's clearly what you hope,
I'll go and d-d-dangle at the noose end of a rope.

Chapter V

NATURAL CURIOSITIES COLLECTED ON JAVA

Ludimus innocuis verbis -- Mart.[183]

I really ought to find space for the corporal's dearly beloved concubine in my cabinet of moral fauna but how could I preserve her? Packing her in butter like a ham would be too expensive for my pocket and it would be impracticable to store her in a bottle since, although I could find one large enough for an ordinary human body, her gigantic breasts would always be hanging outside like a couple of beggar's sacks. Nor can she be transported alive for who knows whether the seamen would break their way into her in her cage?

I must, however, admire the corporal's choice taste for natural curiosities. It makes me convinced that love is not in the least blind as is unjustly supposed since, if he is capable of seeing divine attractions in a monkey, he must have keener sight than Argus.

There are as many monkeys here as there are trees. Linnaeus classifies them along with human beings – something that I have been unable to understand or take seriously for many years. The old fellow is a satirist at times, I thought, and merely intends to give our dandies and their fashion-aping habits a quick swipe across their fur-coats. But now that I have had an opportunity to study the character of monkeys I discover that he has reason in plenty for his classification. They are self-willed creatures, undisciplined and never still, exactly like our busy, mincing little Celadons, apart from the fact that monkeys neither powder themselves nor whistle nor speak French. But they can certainly strut and sniff *en perfection*. I own one and if one of these gentlemen would care to pay me a visit I would make it *salaam* with its hat under its arm as it said: '*Ma foi, monsieur! C'est un joli singe, vous vous ressemblez comme deux gouttes d'eau.*'[184]

I also own a very well-mannered parrot. These are reckoned to be of the avian race but in my opinion they should be classified together with trivial-minded women since they are beautiful, they walk on two legs, they talk almost incessantly and they think a lot of themselves.

We were able to get turtles at a good price. They are very meaty and are a source of healthy food. They resemble seamen to the extent that they thrive best in water and only go ashore to lay eggs and produce young.

I observed a peculiar species of bird of prey that flew over from Java to Sumatra every evening and returned in the morning. I don't know its name. It resembles a raven in size and flight. Its vice in the moral sphere must be ingratitude since it eats its fill abroad and then travels away – just like many of the foreigners in Sweden, who harvest money for a while, ruin half-a-dozen pretty maids and then push off.

There is an animal called a *Waldman* [185] that has a greater resemblance to man than any other animal and is thus thought to be the progeny of some escaped slave-girl who had intercourse with the male great apes.

As I haven't seen a living waldman with my own eyes I am unable to give an account of his moral characteristics and, instead, I should like to put a question to Messrs Naturalist: is it not possible for the crossing of two species to produce a third? Mules stem from horses and donkeys and waldmen are born of men and monkeys; might not a new species of flower result in a similar way from an illicit little love affair between a tulip and a carnation?

I know that a clever gardener can improve his flowers. Without injecting colours into the stems he is able to turn white tulips into multi-coloured varieties by deftly mixing seed. I also know that both France and Spain were inhabited by nothing but cowardly weaklings until our roving Goths and Norsemen began to reinvigorate their insipid races with healthier and bolder blood. New natural products should thus not be impossible.

Which leads me to a splendid thought. Given a successful marriage between *Hat* and *Cap* it should be possible to reproduce that long-lost and sorely missed species *the honest Swede*. The sanguine ambition of the one party moderated by the phlegmatic economy of the other – by which I mean the heart of the Hat united to the head for figures of the Cap – might well spawn a lion which, like the one of old, could scorn both threats from close quarters and bribes from afar.

To dance to the Muscovite bagpipes is cowardly, to hop in step with the French cockerel ridiculous.[186] The first is an old polka, the second a piece of foolish tightrope walking.

Furthermore, dear listeners, furthermore! If you want a good church bell you should cross a smith with a precentor's daughter since his sledgehammer and her Amen harmonise splendidly, and if you want an arch-thief inject a miller into a son who is working in his father's grocery store. I remain etc....

Chapter VI

CONCERNING FRUIT, NUNS, LOOSE LIVING ETC

Nitimur in vetitum -- Ovid.[187]

Bananas are to be found here in great abundance. They grow on trees and hang down like great bunches of thick fingers. They taste excellent but their appearance is not in the least attractive and I never cease to wonder about Eve being led astray by them (for they are generally considered to be the forbidden fruit). Were it not that the inquisitiveness of her daughters convinces me that they must have inherited it from their mother I would have thought that it was hunger alone that seduced her, especially as there is nothing apart from the actual length of the fruit to tickle a woman's fancy.

In Catholic countries where they grow they are served as dessert in nunneries, but they take the peculiar precaution of only sending them in after they have split them open. I don't know why. They are possibly afraid that some St Birgitta might swallow the banana whole.

Oxenstierna says that a beautiful nun is like the forbidden fruit: *Il se trouve toujours quelqu'Adam qui en goute.*[188] I could, if I wished, accuse those of my fellow travellers who had been on Faial [189] of heresy since they have prayed to the bones of saints and said *Ave Maria* while carrying a piece of silken cloth under their arms. What popery!

Coconut trees are tall and devoid of branches right up to the crown on top, in which the nuts hang like huge heads. Osbeck has described their characteristics but he fails to mention how easy it is to catch monkeys in them. I claim that honour. Javanese boys climb up and cut a little hole in the nuts, wide on the outside and narrower within. The monkey comes along and, being inquisitive, sticks its hand in and gets stuck because it has the habit of spreading its fingers out when it wants to jerk itself free. That's what happens to petty thieves. However long they may get away with it they always end up in handcuffs.

This kind of nut often contains a whole tankard of juice. If you wash your head in it and then lie down and sleep in the heat of the sun for a couple of hours, you will acquire beautiful, black full-bodied hair as well as a crazed mind. A certain quartermaster, who was more enamoured of his locks than of his senses, put it to the test and still shows all the signs of his experiment both on the inside and the outside of his head. Poor fool! But perhaps he was a hair's breadth smarter than those women at home who, for the sake of a narrow waist, ruin their health and take the risk of dying in childbirth by lacing themselves so tight that they go round looking like upturned sugarloaves.

Grapefruit is a beautiful and refreshing fruit, greenish-yellow in colour and the size of a cabbage. I have included two of them among my natural curiosities as models of the breasts of Javanese maidens.

Pineapples, the most delicious of all the food in this region, grows in more or less the same way as pine cones at home except that they are much bigger. They are sensuality itself to eat and they have the same effect: that is, they are damaging to the health.

Pepper grows like grass here. The Dutch have taken a complete monopoly on the pepper trade both in Java and on the surrounding islands. They burn huge storehouses of it every year to prevent the price being ruined by an excess of the commodity. What a dog in the manger attitude!

Our excessive consumption of fruit precipitated bowel motions of such power that they threatened to take both cheek-bones and stomachs with them. Had I not resolved to be polite and respectable I would have described how my friends dropped their ballast and pummelled their elbows on the doors of the officers' privies. But I shall hold my tongue and merely offer my condolences to those whose only claim to dignity is to have a big belly; they really suffer. So many visits to the throne equal so many lost points.

Chapter VII

A QUICK HOP OVER TO CHINA

Contigimus portum, quo mihi cursus erat – Ovid.[190]

With only the mildest of breezes to help we dragged ourselves, so to speak, step by step from country to country. There was nothing for it but to keep on dropping and lifting the anchor, partly because of the lack of wind and partly because of the adverse current. The crew was forced to work at the windlass continuously, and the heat sapped them so that progress was slow and toiling. But spurs help the mare and a noggin helps the matelot. No sooner had our captain bade them Huzza for a Lasse than the anchor was off the bottom and the sails set. We lost a kedge anchor one day. Our guess was that it had got caught under a large rock but then we suddenly remembered that a two hundredweight chest of gold had been ditched in the sea at this very spot by a hunted fugitive and we were filled with the hope of netting a rich prize. Greed doubled the seamen's strength and they set to – so vigorously, unfortunately, that the cable snapped and we lost our booty. It's lying there still for the profit of fishermen more fortunate than ourselves.

At last we got a little help from the wind and it took us past Lucipara. The waters in this region are the most difficult of the whole voyage and it was necessary to take soundings the whole way through as there is scarcely four fathoms of water in certain places, which is why a good number of ships have run aground. We had the jolly boat in front plumbing the depth for us and we managed to get through without mishap, passing Monopin on the island of Bangka on the 22nd of August, the sixteenth day after our arrival off Java Head. All we saw of the tin mines of Bangka was the rising fumes of sulphur that spread ash all around. Apart from that, the surrounding islands look like the links in a green and well-wooded chain.

As soon as we reached open sea again the winds became fresh. On the 27th we sighted Poulo-Sapatu – the Shoemaker's Last – a small rock in the middle of the open sea that is all bare apart from being whitewashed by the eggs of innumerable birds. A little earlier we had left Poulo-Condore on our port bow, the island where two Swedish ships – *Kalmar* in 1746 and our own *Finland* in 1764 – had lain over. In the latter case a boat with twenty or more men was lost without anyone knowing how. Since the inhabitants are scarcely more than a pack of pirates suspicion fell on them at first until an intrepid second mate and the purser went ashore to investigate the matter with two loaded blunderbusses on their shoulders. They found no cause for suspicion and thus it was assumed that the men must have been lost in a violent squall.

The mate in question was called Stiernlöf. He has distinguished himself in a number of bold enterprises in the East Indies but I shall pass over him with no comment for the moment as I intend to write a special chapter on those of our East Indiamen who have earned a reputation in some such way.

There are two steady winds that blow in the China Sea, each of them for six months of the year. One of them assists us to reach Canton, the other helps us depart. The horrendous storms known as typhoons in these parts occur when these winds are on the turn. Anyone who reaches the area after September cannot be sure of reaching his destination that year. But we were now sailing along with a brisk southwesterly and dropped anchor off Macao in the Chinese archipelago on the 5th of September. We took pilots aboard and anchored in Whampoa on the 7th of the same month.

Anyone who cares to count how many times the world turned on its axis between the 21st of June and the 7th of September can discover how long it took us from the Cape to Canton. If you are minded to go back to the 24th of December 1769 when we lost sight of the Vinga beacon,[191] you should be able to estimate that we had been away from home for 8 1/2 months.

Continuation of the Fourth Finnish Expedition

Chapter VIII

Impiger extremos currit mercator ad Indos – Horat.[192]

Whampoa, an island where the Europeans have their anchorage, lies about ten miles from Canton and possesses a small town of the same name. We found that the *Prins Gustav* was already there along with thirteen other ships, and a further nine arrived after us, which brought the total of European ships that year to 24 – 13 English, 5 Dutch, 2 French, 2 Danish and our two. In addition to these there was a Portuguese ship anchored in Macao.

On our arrival, we greeted them with eight guns and they all responded in a higgledy-piggledy fashion, which set up a jolly thundering that echoed round the whole district. A ship veiled in powder smoke is amongst the prettiest sights I have seen, especially in fine weather when the smoke spreads in circular, ascending squirls that leave the ship, so to speak, floating in cloud. Had there been human heads flying about I could have imagined we were in the midst of a sea battle, there being no shortage of explosions as well as the screaming and waving of arms as the hundreds of Chinese sampans that were thronging around the ships set off in great haste for the paddy fields to the accompaniment of tremulous cries.

The sight of this many large, well-manned ships is a truly impressive one. The Europeans, who are so keen to argue among themselves when at home, live together like fellow-countrymen here and only compete in terms of showing respect for each other. This deserves a paean if I can manage one. We shall see!

Chapter IX

A SWIPE AT THE JESUITS

It is beyond my ability to give a proper description of this place, nor do I aim to do so since little could be achieved by any such attempt in respect of a country where one is ignorant of the language and forbidden to wander beyond certain streets. It would do nothing but add a couple more handfuls of untruths to the enormous mass of lies that has already been exported to Europe along with pottery and chests of China tea.

People have written strange and wonderful things about China. Its inhabitants are supposed to be as old as the earth itself and their profusion is only to be compared with that of the stars. Confucius, if we are to believe the missionaries, surpasses not only Mohammed but even Moses and Paul. The honour of Rome, the virtue of Sparta and the wisdom of Athens have flowed together in one place – in almighty Peking. Their government is beyond compare, their laws divine, their customs paragon. In short, all the wisdom of Solomon is to be found resting on a shaven Chinese head.

What is the foundation on which the Jesuits have built these castles in the air? I shan't say it was on the basis of their gratitude for ready Chinese cash since sordid self-interest could surely not have influenced their apostolic souls? It might well, however, have been for the honour of their religion. Just imagine how much that honour is increased by the supposed conquest of such a large and unparalleled empire! Imagine the scope for selling indulgences, imagine the church taxes from mighty China! So it should be clear to everyone that they had good reasons to spread their songs in praise of this country!

I have no desire at all to undermine the credibility of their descriptions but I detest an historian who overwhelms me with panegyrics when all I'm expecting is a narrative. Canton is claimed to be the most remarkable place in China after Peking. If that is so, why should I have failed to find any trace of its highly praised splendours – if they are real? I must therefore conclude that the holy Jesuit fathers have lavished their paeans on China just so that the echo of their own prowess might ring all the more loudly in Europe, whereas their reputation as apostles might have been diminished had the proselytes been less impressive.

As a result of this I have no intention of describing anything from here though I shall, if I may, toss out one or two remarks about things in general in a couple of short chapters. I promise to be on my best behaviour and not to try to press my opinions on others.

Craftsmen, merchants and a host of mandarins are the only people that Europeans in Canton may come in contact with and their story is not worth the effort of writing it. Mr P. Osbeck is the Swedish traveller who has described in most detail what he came across here. I thus refer any serious-minded reader to his book and would merely add the justified recommendation that his pen has been guided by the truth as far as I can judge.

Chapter X

CONCERNING INCORRECT ADDITION

When travellers ascribe to China a population of sixty million between the ages of twenty and sixty alone I think they must be counting both two and four-legged creatures. How else could it be comprehensible? Consider the actual size of the country and tell me where this enormous number could be accommodated and, if you could rent space for them, what you are going to feed them on. The whole of the northern part consists, when all is said and done, of mountains and forest; and the rest cannot be any more than ordinarily fertile, unless you claim that China has been exempted from the ordinary decrees of this earth. Are they supposed to be able to eat rocks and trees or do quails and manna rain down into their mouths as happened to Moses in the desert? Europe, most of it at least, is well cultivated but even then it is necessary to find food in other parts of the world either by trade or emigration. Would China alone, then, be able to feed as many inhabitants as all of our populous European states together?

There are, besides, numerous considerations that make this whole business debatable. Their unnatural taste for sodomite love, their laws (which do not oblige a husband to visit his wife more than once a year if he so wishes), the right to expose their children, the rapid aging of their womenfolk (which either makes them incapable of breeding beyond their thirtieth year or frightens their men away); all this, together with the wars and rebellions which are almost invariably on the go in one or other of the distant provinces, makes it highly unlikely.

Their polygamy and the fact that they rarely migrate abroad might be thought to balance this out. But these, especially the former, hardly provide a counterweight. You only have to compare the population of Europe with that of the Orient in order to see how little effect polygamy has on the increase of the species. Is not Germany more populous than Turkey relative to the area of the two countries? When was a Persian woman ever so prolific a childbearer as a European woman? No, if you want your homeland filled with healthy people, give each woman her own husband for, when we have too much to take care of, the result will never be more than bungled work.

As to the second point, it is true that the Chinese usually remain in their homeland; nor are they permitted to do otherwise since emigration is strictly forbidden. It is impossible for a European to get men here even if he needs them, unless he deposits sound financial guarantees that he will bring them all back again. One example of this was an English captain whose whole crew had jumped ship. This wise regulation on the part of the state must certainly increase the population count and I would have accepted it as the main reason were it not that I know of 80 000 exceptions to it in Batavia and probably as many again on the coasts of Japan. The Chinese make up half the population of the former and trade has encouraged a good many to move over to the latter, not to mention the fact that many people here and elsewhere perish at sea.

What reason, then, can travellers from Europe have for inventing such a large population in China? The answer, I guess, is simply that the majority of the travellers have seen just a couple of the grandest cities in the empire – Peking, Canton or Nanking, for instance – and have judged the rest of the country by that measure: seven square miles of Nanking contains a million people, the whole of China equals seven hundred square miles, therefore there are 100 million Chinese. What a flood of figures, and how fortunate that they are no more than figures! The globe would otherwise run the risk of instant inundation. The Emperor's naval power is reckoned to consist of 9,999 sails and I imagine that the reason for that is simply that four nines go very nicely together!

I do not deny that it is easy to be deceived on first arriving in Canton, for instance. You are no sooner inside the Tiger's Mouth [193] than the country opens out in a great wide-stretched circle full of small towns, villages and pagodas and surrounded by pretty green hills and fertile flat farmland. The river as it runs on to Canton contains all sorts of big and small islands that resemble pleasure gardens, and it also supports what might be called a floating republic of innumerable sampans lined up into veritable streets close to the town itself. All this gives me a grand conception of the place and I conclude – quite reasonably – that there is an enormous multitude of people. But when I consider that Canton is the meeting place of pretty well the whole province and that people stream there from all directions during the European trading season as though to a public market, then the miracle loses its conviction. You have to elbow your way through the throng at the St Lawrence Market in Gothenburg but I would not want to estimate the population of the town from it. A good proportion of the sampans belong far up-country and the merchants in Amoy, where the Europeans used to do their trading, have now moved down here. The market attracts the swarms to come there but, once the ships have left, the outskirts of Canton

– which is where most of the activity takes place – are almost empty.

The place is superbly cultivated, however, as it is bound to be given the millions of European pieces-of-eight that are buried every year. But don't let us go on inventing Chinese *ad infinitum.* I can't give you the right number but I am sure that there is no basis for it being 60 million counting only healthy adults and excluding people under 20 and over 60 years of age.

NOTES

1. Horace, *Ars Poetica*, 139. 'Mountains are in labour [and a laughable little mouse is born].' The second half of the line heads Book 1, Chapter III.
2. The allusions are to a variety of contemporary events: a) *L---* refers to Daniel (L)jungmarker (1726-72), mason and parliamentary representative for Gothenburg, who was accused of using procedural tricks to support his views on constitutional change b) *Colonel P-* is Carl Fredrik Pechlin (1720-96), who changed sides in the parliament of 1769-70 because of his opposition to increased royal authority c) *Swedenborgian spirits* refers to a case in 1769-1770 in which two Swedenborgians were brought before the ecclesiastical court on a charge of heresy d) *Khotin*, now in the southern Ukraine, was then a Turkish fortress captured in 1769 by the Russian Field Marshal A.M. Golitsyn (1718-83) during the Russo-Turkish War of 1768-74 e) the reference to London, which Wallenberg had visited earlier in 1769, is one of several sallies against the city he described as 'the ugliest town I have ever seen'.
3. 'People may drink wine, other creatures drink from springs.' According to Afzelius, the motto is not from Ovid and probably not from a classical source at all.
4. Lilla Klippan, an inn in the Majorna district of Gothenburg close to the East India Company stores and consequently popular with company staff, was run 1768-70 by James Carnegie (1740-1810), one of the many Scots to be found in Gothenburg and the west coast of Sweden from the 16th century onwards. Masthugget is now a district of central Gothenburg.
5. 'Howl with the wolves if you want to be with them.' Latin proverb.
6. There have been a series of fortresses at Älvsborg since the Middle Ages to defend the mouth of the Göta River. The importance of the herring fishing industry was such that the firing of cannon for ceremonial purposes was prohibited at certain periods.
7. Peter Wessel Tordenskiold (1690-1720) was the Norwegian naval officer who led the Danish fleet in its mainly successful attacks on the Swedish west coast in 1719.
8. Carl von Linné (Linnaeus) (1707-78), the great Swedish botanist whose *Systema naturae* was printed in 1735. Wallenberg makes a number of references to him and his disciples and on various occasions (eg. Book 1,

Chapter XVII) playfully parodies scientific travel-writing. R.A. Ferchault de Reaumur (1683-1757) and G.L.L.Buffon (1707-88) were renowned French natural scientists.

9. Virgil, *Bucolics*, I.3. 'We flee our native land and leave the pleasant fields.'

10. Olof Rudbeck the Elder (1630-1702), Swedish natural scientist and antiquarian, published his *Atland eller Manheim* in four volumes from 1679 to 1702. He claims Sweden to be the most ancient kingdom in the world and traces its origin to Japheth, son of Noah. *Atland* became a common poetic synonym for Sweden.

11. Louis XV (1710-74), King of France.

12. The Hats and the Caps were the two political parties that competed for power in the Swedish Riksdag during the Age of Freedom (1718-72).

13. Virgil, *Aeneid*, V.481. 'The ox falls to the ground.'

14. 'To call upon Ulrich' is an onomatopoeic Swedish expression (borrowed from German) for 'to vomit'.

15. Adaptation of a line from Ovid, *Heroides*, XVII.253. 'Your body is more suited to Ceres [agriculture] than to Mars [war].' The original has Venus instead of Ceres.

16. M.Bret, *Memoires sur la vie de mademoiselle de Lenclos* (1758). 'Love lives in storms.'

17. A French expedition was in Swedish Lapland during the winter of 1736-37 to carry out measurements of latitude. It ascertained that the earth flattened out at the Poles. The leader of the expedition, Pierre Louis Maupertuis (1698-1759), fell in love with Christina Planström, daughter of a town councillor in Torneå, and wrote verses in her praise, of which this is one. The girl's head was clearly turned since she and her younger sister Elisabeth followed the expedition back to France never to return north. Christina's fate was to end up out of her mind in a nunnery whereas Elisabeth made an unsuccessful marriage to a nobleman. The Swedish translation of the poem was, as Wallenberg rightly says, made by Anders Celsius (1701-44), inventor of the centigrade temperature scale and instigator of the Lapland expedition.

18. From the preface to the Roman historian Cornelius Nepos' *Vitae excellentium imperatorum*. 'I have no doubt that many will consider [my manner of writing to be simple].'

19. *Glossarium Suio-Gothicum* (1769), a major etymological dictionary by the Swede Johan Ihre (1707-80).

20. ie. English 'mate'.

21. It is not possible to reflect the Swedish pun in English. *Dagg* can mean both 'dew' and 'rope's end'.
22. A description by K.N.Lenaeus of the parish of Delsbo (1764).
23. Virgil, *Aeneid*, I.87. 'Then follow the shouts of the sailors and the creaking of cables.'
24. The reference is to the story of the destruction of Jerusalem as narrated in the contemporary Swedish book of psalms.
25. Virgil, *Aeneid*, III.658. 'Like a horrible monster, formless, ugly...'
26. Ovid, *Metamorphoses*, XI.537-38. 'As many deaths seem rushing on and bursting through as are the advancing waves.'
27. Otterhällan is a hill in Gothenburg and Hisingen an island that is now part of the city.
28. Trollhättan Falls were a major waterfall on the Göta River. As a result of hydro-electric works, they are now usually dry.
29. Pehr Schenberg (1707-77), *Lexicon Latino-Svecanum*.
30. Karl XII (1682-1718), the warrior king whose continuous campaigning failed to retain for Sweden her position as a major European power and ultimately led the country to war weariness and near bankruptcy. He nevertheless became a national hero. It is not beyond the bounds of possibility that the bullet that killed him came from his own side. Wallenberg's reference is incorrect; it should be to Karl's crossing from Karlhamn to Pernau in 1700.
31. Virgil, *Aeneid*, X.115. 'With a nod [Jupiter] makes Olympus tremble.'
32. A free quotation from Isaiah 66:1.
33. Propertius, *Elegies*, II.1.43. 'The seaman describes the winds, the ploughman his ox.'
34. Latin proverb. 'He who cannot pray may go to sea.'
35. Horace, *Ars Poetica*, 1-2. 'If a painter dared to place a human head on a horse's neck...'
36. It is Menelaus who is compared to a fly in *Iliad*, XVII.570-73.
37. The Danish dramatist and historian Ludvig Holberg (1684-1754) makes the comparison between the Danish King Christian IV (1577-1648) and the Swedish Gustavus Adolphus (1594-1632) in his *History of the Kingdom of Denmark*.
38. Kungsbacka, a small town south of Gothenburg, was going through bad times in the 18th century and had had its trading charter withdrawn from 1724 to 1766.

39. A free quotation not from Ovid but Virgil, *Aeneid*, V.6. 'You do not know what a [furious] woman is capable of.'
40. Ebba Brahe (1596-1674), mistress of Gustavus Adolphus. The latter's mother prevented their marriage.
41. Not Ovid but Virgil, *Bucolics*, X.69. 'Love conquers all.'
42. Virgil, *Aeneid*, II.34. 'Thus fate ordained it for Troy.'
43. Close to the southern tip of Norway.
44. ie. Cervantes' Don Quixote.
45. Horace, *Odes*, I.6.17. 'We sing of feasts and of the battles of maidens.'
46. 'A lady to his taste.'
47. 'To what purpose?'
48. Anders Nicander (1707-81), a poetaster in both Swedish and Latin.
49. A free quotation from Horace, *Epistles*, II.2.2. 'The seller praises the wares he wishes to pass off.'
50. Norway was subject to Denmark from the Middle Ages until 1814.
51. Parts of western Pomerania belonged to Sweden from 1648 to 1814 at which date, by the Treaty of Kiel, they were exchanged for Norway.
52. Sweden has had a law on press freedom since 1766.
53. Virgil, *Aeneid*, III.26. 'A wonder it is to relate.'
54. A play on the title of a well-known illustrated schoolbook *Orbis Pictus* by J.A. Comenius (1592-1670).
55. 'for better, for worse.'
56. Öland is 85 miles long.
57. Erik Pontopiddan (1698-1764), Bishop of Bergen, gives an account of the kraken in his *First Attempt at the Natural History of Norway*.
58. Job 40-41.
59. A reference to Swedish lack of success in the 1757-62 war with Prussia.
60. Ovid, *Tristia*, IV.1.3. 'I was an exile and sought not fame but rest.'
61. J.B.Brelin, author of a travel narrative (1758) dealing with the East Indies, South America and Europe. He was accidentally left behind on Ascension Island, was suspected of having deserted and eventually made his way back to Sweden. Pehr Osbeck (1723-1805) was a botanist and disciple of Linnaeus; he wrote an account of a journey to the East Indies as a ship's chaplain. Olof Torén (d.1753), likewise a ship's chaplain, described his voyage to the East Indies in letters to Linnaeus.
62. Julius Caesar Scaliger (1484-1558), Dutch philologist.
63. Roman authors of works on grammar and rhetoric respectively.
64. Pliny the Younger, *Epistles*, IX.26.

65. Horace, *Epistles*, I.10.24. 'If you drive nature out with a pitchfork she will soon find a way back.'
66. Paul Scarron (1610-60), French satirist and author of *Le roman comique*. Thomas Hobbes (1588-1679), English philosopher.
67. Ovid, *Tristia*, II.18. 'The battered ship returns to the surging sea.'
68. The ship had lost 60 of its crew during the previous voyage.
69. A free quotation from Ovid, *Tristia*, I.5.17. 'It [the ship] is now driven by a favourable wind.'
70. Horace, *Epistles*, I.5.19. 'Who did not become eloquent from full goblets?'
71. Circe was celebrated in Greek mythology for her knowledge of magic and poisonous potions. Ulysses visited her while returning from the Trojan War and his companions, who hurled themselves into voluptuousness at her court, were turned into swine by her potions.
72. John Wilkes (1727-97), English politician and favourite of the London mob. His suspension from Parliament and imprisonment for libel in 1768 led to rioting.
73. Horace, *Ars Poetica*, 356. 'He is laughed at who always blunders on the same string.'
74. Maecenas was a celebrated Roman who was a liberal patron and friend of literary men including Virgil and Horace.
75. German: 'The Journeyman Tailors' Inn.'
76. Fulmar.
77. 'The terrible jaws crave for all that sea and land and air can furnish.' The second part of the quotation is Ovid, *Metamorphoses*, VIII.830-31.
78. 'Garbage eater.'
79. 'The law of the talon', ie. an eye for an eye, a tooth for a tooth.
80. Skagen is the northernmost point of Denmark.
81. Diogenes (c.410-c.320 BC), Greek philosopher and one of the founders of the Cynics. His asceticism and scorn for niceties led him to live in a barrel.
82. Virgil, *Aeneid*, I.1. 'Arms and the man I sing.'
83. The heroine and title figure of a popular German romantic adventure novel (1689) by Heinrich von Ziegler und Klipphausen.
84. A free quotation from Voltaire's *Henriade*, VIII.381 (1728). 'The French know how to win and to sing of their victories.'
85. A London prison and workhouse.
86. Ovid, *Tristia*, V.1.74. 'I composed among the Sarmatians.'

87. Johan Runius (1679-1713), an excellent poet particularly of funeral and wedding odes and bacchanalian verses. Undoubtedly the most popular poet of his age, he enjoyed a considerable reputation for Bohemian living.
88. Virgil, *Aeneid*, I.734. 'May Bacchus, giver of joy, be present.'
89. A free quotation from Ovid, *Amores*, III.11.5. 'We trample love beneath our feet.'
90. John Wilmot (1647-80), Earl of Rochester. He led a life of debauchery and produced much amatory and bacchanalian poetry until 'saved' by Bishop Burnet (see note 168).
91. Dog Latin. 'Whether it is right or wrong it is Latin anyway.'
92. 'Each has his own taste.'
93. Horace, *Epistles*, I.4.16. 'A hog from Epicurus' herd.'
94. 'Oh, what a mortal blow for the drinking brothers in our happy company! Farewell, bottle, farewell, my life! Behold thy secretary in tears! Bacchus, all thy loyal subjects who have demonstrated thy power with courage and loyalty will no longer sacrifice at thine altar!'
95. Virgil, *Bucolics*, III.111. 'Close now the channels, lads, the meadows have had enough to drink!'
96. Latin proverb. 'As the king, so the common herd.'
97. *Henriette* (1758) by Charlotte Lennox (1720-1804). An anonymous Swedish translation appeared in 1782 and Afzelius suggests this might have been Captain Ekeberg's work.
98. A free quotation from Ovid, *Tristia*, V.10.38. 'The stupid Getae laugh at my Latin words.'
99. Admiral George Anson (1697-1762) left England with six ships in 1740 as commander of the Pacific Squadron and returned with only one ship in 1744, having circumnavigated the globe.
100. Virgil, *Aeneid*, III.530. 'A favourable wind blows up and a harbour opens out.'
101. Horace, *Ars Poetica*, 322. 'Empty verses and fine-sounding bagatelles.'
102. 'Money, Sirs, money!'
103. Ovid, *Ex Ponto*, I.3.35. 'I do not know with what sweet power our homeland draws us all and does not allow us to forget it.'
104. Ludvig Holberg, *Third Epistle*, p.319.
105. Virgil, *Aeneid*, I.67. 'A people I detest sails on the Tyrrhenian Sea.'
106. The opening of Cornelius Nepos' *Vitae excellentium imperatorum*. 'Miltiades the Athenian, son of Cimon.'

107. The opening sentence of C.S.Hedman's *Grammatica Latina contracta* (1745). 'Grammar is the art of speaking and writing.'
108. Source unknown. 'Oh, how terrible the foolish mob seems to me.'
109. Christian von Wolff (1679-1754), German philosopher and mathematician. A supporter of rationalism, he was one of the main philosophers of the Enlightenment in Germany.
110. A *Theologia moralis* by Cervantes is unknown.
111. Carl Michael Bellman (1740-95), Swedish poet and songwriter whose works are still enormously popular. His best known works are *Fredman's Epistles* and *Fredman's Songs* which treat love, drink, decay and death with a mixture of bawdy humour and rococo charm.
112. 4th century Roman grammarian whose works became the standard textbooks through the Middle Ages and later.
113. Latin proverb. 'Natural things are not disgusting.'
114. A free quotation from Virgil, *Aeneid*, VI.258. 'Away from here, away, unhallowed ones!'
115. The first part of a Latin proverb. 'A little of everything, [nothing completely].'
116. Horace, *Satires*, I.1.29-30. 'Seamen who boldly voyage around all the oceans.'
117. Virgil, *Aeneid*, I.204. 'Through various events, through innumerable dangers.'
118. In Swedish folklore, the hill to which witches resort on broomsticks in order to meet their Satanic master on the night of Maundy Thursday.
119. Genesis 7:11.
120. German: 'The sky is sweating.'
121. Matthew 17:20.
122. Clement XIV. He was pope from 1769 to 1774 and in 1773 he made universal the partial suppression of the Jesuits that Wallenberg refers to in Book 3 Chapter 12.
123. Olof von Dalin (1708-63), Swedish author and the most important literary figure of the Age of Freedom. His weekly journal *Then Swänska Argus* (1732-34) with its moralising essays and satires marks both the the arrival of the Enlightenment in Sweden and the modern period in Swedish language history.The quotation is from his 'Song about Pepper'.
124. Ovid, *Tristia*, III.7.43. 'We own nothing that is not mortal.'
125. A free quotation from Virgil, *Aeneid*, II.6-8. 'Who could hold back tears when he tells of such a thing.'

126. A king in ancient Greece, Croesus was accounted the richest of men; Irus, on the other hand, was a beggar who appears in Homer's *Odyssey*.
127. Maevius was an inferior Roman poet ridiculed by the great Virgil (Virgillius Maro).
128. Martial XI.6.7. 'We may say whatever occurs to us.'
129. Linnaeus mentions Tulbagh with appreciation on a number of occasions and writes that 'he sent me over 200 of the rarest plants, very well packed, as well as an abundance of living roots and bulbs to be planted in gardens.'
130. 'At the feet of his brown beauty.'
131. The Edict of Nantes (1598) had guaranteed the Protestant Huguenots in France freedom of worship. Its revocation in 1685 led to large-scale emigration.
132. The priest in question was, of course, Wallenberg himself. Afzelius reports an anecdote about the sermon and the payment for it which shows Wallenberg in a light that will not perhaps come as a surprise to his readers. It seems that Wallenberg would have received a fee twice as big had the strict congregation not discovered him at cards after the service was over.
133. A free quotation from Ovid, *Ars Amatoria*, I.757. 'The same sort of earth cannot produce everything.'
134. André Le Nôtre (1613-1700), French landscape gardener whose masterpiece is the gardens at Versailles.
135. 'A little cup of tea, sir.'
136. 'Good Appetite, Cheers, Good Health.'
137. A free quotation from Ludvig Holberg, *Third Epistle*, p.324.
138. J.T.Oxenstierna (1666-1733), member of a leading Swedish aristocratic family. He absconded from his tutor at the age of 16 while in Germany on his educational journey and spent the next 40 years wandering Europe. His literary work consists largely of aphorisms and essays written in French. This is a free quotation from his *Pensées de divers sujets de morale*, I.118. 'It is a country where the demon of money is crowned with tobacco and sits on a throne of cheese.'
139. Ovid, *Amores*, III.12.16. 'Corinna alone has inspired me.'
140. A free quotation from Ovid, *Ars Amatoria*, III.321. 'He [Orpheus] moved stones and wild animals with his lyre.'
141. Batavia was the Dutch colonial name for Jakarta.
142. The Amarant Order was founded by Queen Kristina in 1653 and its motto means 'Sweet shall be the memory thereof'.

143. Not Horace but Perseus, *Satires*, IV.51. 'Reject what you are not.'
144. From a 17th century student song. 'Fiddlers, scrape your fiddles.'
145. Virgil, *Aeneid*, IV.165-66. 'Dido and the leader of the Trojans came to the same cave.'
146. 'Charming creature...I lie not... I love you with all my heart...give me a kiss for my dog...my dear...Oh, sir, you are a rogue...the love of East Indiamen is not to be trusted...go, go, no more...I have given you two...-No,no, my sweet maid, you have promised me seven kisses...you must pay for the dog...one more...that was good...one more, one more...one more...good maid...What? Are you not ashamed? I'll get angry...you're smearing my mouth...fie, you haven't shaved today...how many kisses am I supposed to give you for the dog?...sh, sh, you madman...go, go, my mother is coming.'
147. 'I wish I could sleep as well as my dog tonight.'
148. Sigonius and Hasenskräck are the names of the main characters in the Swedish translation of Ludvig Holberg's play *Jacob von Tyboe*. Sigonius is the arrogant pedant and Hasenskräck the braggart warrior.
149. *Ziektrooster* = 'deacon'; *myn Confrater* = 'my colleague'.
150. 'For spiritual care on their ships.'
151. A play on Deuteronomy 25:4. 'Thou shalt not muzzle the ox when he treadeth out the corn.'
152. A reference to Jesus' statement to Pilate in John 18:36. 'My kingdom is not of this world.'
153. A play on Virgil, *Bucolics*, III.60. 'Everything is full of ox.' The original has 'Jove' for 'ox'.
154. A free quotation from Virgil, *Aeneid*, XII.722. 'The whole grove echoes with the bellowing of oxen.'
155. Refers to the ban imposed on the Jesuits by a number of Catholic monarchs in the 1750s and 1760s.
156. Latin proverb. 'Women's weeping bodes deceit.'
157. 'The laurels stick up between the horns.'
158. Horace, *Ars Poetica*, 413. 'The boy has endured much and done much.'
159. Virgil, *Aeneid*, I.135. 'I will show you...!' The phrase was often used as a humorous threat.
160. A free quotation bringing together two separate couplets from Haquin Spegel's *The Open Paradise* (1705). Bishop Spegel (1645-1714) - he became archbishop towards the end of his life - was one of the great hymn writers and psalmists as well as the compiler of the first printed Swedish dictionary.

161. Not from Cornelius Nepos but from Horace, *Odes*, IV.4.29. 'The sturdy are born of the sturdy.'
162. 'I'm not going to pay that much for repentance.' Reputed to be the words of the philosopher Demosthenes when he heard what the famous courtesan Lais of Corinth proposed to charge him for a night in her bed.
163. A play on Matthew 19.6. 'What therefore God hath joined together, let not guardian put asunder.' The original has 'man' not 'guardian'.
164. 'Strength and security from this.'
165. Asmodeus is an evil spirit in the Apocryphal Book of Tobit He was an enemy of marital harmony.
166. Cicero, *In Catilinam*, I.1. 'O what times, O what habits!'
167. From Dalin's 'Petition to the Major of the Guard on behalf of the author's servant Petter who has been enlisted as a soldier'. The story of Balaam's ass speaking when its master beat it for stopping before an angel of the Lord is to be found in Numbers 22:22-35.
168. Gilbert Burnet (1643-1715), Scottish churchman and church historian, Bishop of Salisbury. The anecdote is taken from the collection *Joe Miller's Jests* (London, 1739) which seems to have been well known in Sweden.
169. The story of how King David took the young maiden Abishag to warm his old age is in I Kings 1:1-4.
170. The reference is to 2 Kings 4:38-41.
171. In *Paradise Lost*, VI.461ff., Milton has Satan invent artillery.
172. Virgil, *Aeneid*, VII.312. '[If I cannot move the gods of heaven] I shall call upon the underworld.'
173. Virgil, *Aeneid*, I.152-58. 'Tired and with failing strength Aeneas and his men now strive for the nearest shores.'
174. Pasquale de Paoli (1725-1807), Corsican patriot who resisted the take-over of the island by the French in 1768 and was forced to flee to England.
175. Ecclesiastes 1:2.
176. J.T.Oxenstierna, *Pensées sur divers sujets de morale*, I.22.
177. Part of a line from Horace, *Epistles*, I.14.43. 'The ox desires the saddle, [the horse when lazy longs to plough.]'
178. Horace, *Satires*, I.4.34. 'Give him a wide berth, he has hay on his horns.' A reference to the custom of tying hay to the horns of an angry bull.
179. 'Raath van Indien' = 'Council of India'.
180. Genesis 9:27.
181. The incident occurred in 1746 and is mentioned in other accounts, including English ones.

182. Latin proverb. 'He who loves the frog considers her to be Diana.'
183. Martial VII.12.9. 'My jests are harmless.'
184. 'Truly, sir, it's a pretty monkey, and you are as alike as two drops of water.'
185. German: 'man of the woods', ie. orang-utan.
186. He is referring to the pro-Russian tendencies of the Caps and the pro-French tendencies of the Hats.
187. Ovid, *Amores*, III.4.17. 'We strive for that which is forbidden.'
188. A free quotation from J.T.Oxenstierna, *Pensées sur divers sujet de morale*, II.221. 'There is always some Adam who will taste it.'
189. Faial is an island in the Azores. Afzelius suggests that what Wallenberg means is that the seamen attempted to win favour with the nuns with gifts of silk.
190. Ovid, *Remedia amoris*, 812. 'We have reached the harbour to which our journey aimed.'
191. An island off Gothenburg that marks the entry to the main shipping lane to the port.
192. Horace, *Epistles*, I.1.45. 'The merchant travels diligently all the way to the Indies.'
193. The mouth of the Pearl River, on which Canton is situated.

BIBLIOGRAPHICAL NOTE

The present translation follows the critical edition produced by Nils Afzelius in his *Jacob Wallenbergs Samlade Skrifter* (Svenska författare utg. av Svenska Vitterhetssamfundet, 13:1-2, 1928-41) and anyone familiar with that edition will at once recognise my debt to its excellent commentary and notes. The most useful major article on *My Son on the Galley* is also by Afzelius: '*Min son på galejan* och den komiska reseberättelsen', *Samlaren*, 1924, pp.198-234. *Samlade Skrifter* also contains a complete Wallenberg bibliography up to 1941. This has been brought up to date by Sven G. Sjöberg, 'Jacob Wallenberg. Bibliografisk förteckning 1942-82', *Linköpings Biblioteks Handlingar*, N.S.11, 1986, pp.73-86.

Very little by or about Wallenberg has appeared in English apart from the following: Michael Roberts, 'The Travels of a Busybody at the Cape, Being Abstracts from Jacob Wallenberg's *Min son på galejan*', *Quarterly Bulletin of the South African Library*, 1947:2, pp.36-49 and 1948:2, pp.69-75; Steven John Barker, *Wallenberg and his English Contemporaries. A Study in Affinities*, Seattle 1980, 181pp., unpublished dissertation; Peter Graves, 'Jacob Wallenberg, His Galley and a Digression on Literary Histories', *Swedish Book Review*, 1989:2, pp.20-40 (with extracts from *My Son on the Galley* and *A True Account of a Journey*).